SNAPREVISE

SnapRevise Text Guide:
Great Expectations
by Charles Dickens

Gisele Forsyth

InStudent Education UK Ltd owner of SnapRevise® trademark.
43 Priston Close, Worle, BS22 7FL, Weston-Super-Mare, United Kingdom

www.snaprevise.co.uk

Copyright © InStudent Publishing Pty Ltd 2024

All rights reserved. These notes are protected by copyright owned by InStudent Publishing Pty Ltd and you may not reproduce, disseminate, or communicate to the public the whole or a substantial part thereof except as permitted at law or with the prior written consent of InStudent Publishing Pty Ltd.

Title: Great Expectations by Charles Dickens Text Guide
ISBN: 978-1-917424-21-9

Published by InStudent Education UK Ltd CN 15550989 under licence from InStudent Publishing Pty Ltd.
ACN 624 188101

Disclaimer

No reliance on warranty. These SnapRevise materials are intended to supplement but are not intended to replace or to be any substitute for your regular school attendance, for referring to prescribed texts, or for your own note taking. You are responsible for following the appropriate syllabus, attending school classes, and maintaining good study practices. It is your responsibility to evaluate the accuracy of any information, opinions, and advice in these materials. Under no circumstance will InStudent Publishing Pty Ltd or InStudent Education UK Ltd ("Publishers"), their officers, agents, or employees be liable for any loss or damage caused by your use or reliance on these materials, including any adverse impact upon your performance in any academic subject as a result of your use or reliance on the materials. You accept that all information provided or made available by the Publishers is in the nature of general information and does not constitute advice. It is not guaranteed to be error-free and you should always independently verify any information, including through use of a professional teacher and other reliable resources. To the extent permissible at law, the Publishers expressly disclaim all warranties or guarantees of any kind, whether express or implied, including without limitation any warranties concerning the accuracy or content of information provided in these materials or other fitness for purpose. The Publishers shall not be liable for any direct, indirect, special, incidental, consequential or punitive damages of any kind. You agree to indemnify the Publishers, its officers, agents, and employees against any loss whatsoever by using these materials.

Preface

Hello English students! My name is Gisele Forsyth. I graduated in 2022 and have since started a Bachelor of Fine Arts (Theatre) at the Victorian College of the Arts. During my final years of high school, Literature was one of my favourite subjects, and as such I am no stranger to writing a passage analysis and an essay or two. So, speaking from experience, I recognise that sometimes it can be hard to get started when encountering a new text. However, don't worry – that is where this Text Guide comes in!

Before I read the monumental work, *Great Expectations*, I always thought that studying a Dickensian text would be on par with learning a whole new language. Yet, whilst it did seem like an intimidating novel to cover at first, there are so many key themes and threads that emerge, making it genuinely engaging and interesting to both write about and read.

I found Dickens' strong attentiveness to the social conditions of 19th century England to be a critical focal point for contextualising the narrative. Another element that caught my attention was Dickens' distinct linguistic style, which to me was a compelling component to analyse and discuss. As well as this, his use of satire, hyperbolic descriptions, and elaborate characterisation makes the world of *Great Expectations* come to life, not to mention the plot twists and revelations towards the end of the novel!

In saying this, it really doesn't matter if you're a die-hard Dickens fan or if you just want to get good marks for an essay on *Great Expectations*, I'm sure there will be something in this Text Guide that you will find useful in your studies.

— Gisele Forsyth

Contents

1 **Nutshell Summary** 1
2 **Background Information** 3
   Charles Dickens 3
   19th century England 4
      Society 4
      Gender 6
3 **Chapter-by-Chapter Analysis** 7
   Part 1 7
      Chapter 1 7
      Chapter 2 8
      Chapter 3 9
      Chapter 4 10
      Chapter 5 11
      Chapter 6 11
      Chapter 7 11
      Chapter 8 12
      Chapter 9 14
      Chapter 10 14
      Chapter 11 15
      Chapter 12 16
      Chapter 13 17
      Chapter 14 17
      Chapter 15 18
      Chapter 16 19
      Chapter 17 19
      Chapter 18 20
      Chapter 19 22
   Part 2 23
      Chapter 20 23
      Chapter 21 23
      Chapter 22 24
      Chapters 23, 24, 25, and 26 25
      Chapter 27 25
      Chapter 28 27
      Chapter 29 27
      Chapter 30 28
      Chapter 31 29
      Chapter 32 29

	Chapter 33	29
	Chapter 34	30
	Chapter 35	30
	Chapter 36	30
	Chapter 37	31
	Chapter 38	32
	Chapter 39	33
	Part 3	35
	Chapter 40	35
	Chapter 41	35
	Chapter 42	35
	Chapter 43	36
	Chapter 44	37
	Chapter 45	37
	Chapter 46	38
	Chapter 47	38
	Chapter 48	38
	Chapter 49	39
	Chapters 50, 51, and 52	39
	Chapter 53	40
	Chapter 54	40
	Chapter 55	41
	Chapter 56	41
	Chapter 57	41
	Chapter 58	42
	Chapter 59	43
4	**Character Analysis**	**44**
	Pip	44
	Miss Havisham	45
	Estella	46
	Abel Magwitch	47
	Joe Gargery	47
	Mrs Joe	48
	Biddy	48
	Mr Jaggers	49
	Herbert Pocket	49
	Wemmick	50
	Dolge Orlick	50
	Compeyson	50
	Uncle Pumblechook	51
	Bentley Drummle	51

	Minor characters	52
	Startop	52
	Mr Wopsle	52
	Mr Wopsle's great-aunt	52
	Matthew Pocket	52
	Mrs Pocket	52
	Molly	52
	Arthur Havisham	52
5	**Key Themes Analysis**	**53**
	Social class	53
	Morality and ethics	54
	Ambition	55
	Etiquette	56
	Loyalty, friendship, and genuine human relationships	57
	Manipulation	58
	Desire and objectification	58
6	**Structural Features Analysis**	**60**
	Symbolism	60
	Darkness and light	60
	The weather and physical environment	61
	Time	61
	Estella and the jewels	62
	The "dog-like" simile	62
7	**Quote Bank**	**63**
	Social class	63
	Morality and ethics	65
	Ambition	65
	Etiquette	66
	Loyalty, friendship, and genuine human relationships	67
	Manipulation, desire, and objectification	69
8	**Sample Essays**	**70**
	Essay One	70
	Essay Two	75
	Essay Three	79
	Essay Four	83

Section 1

Nutshell Summary

Great Expectations by Charles Dickens is an epic novel that **trenchantly** explores themes of identity, social class, ambition, and morality. Set in 19th century England, the narrative follows the life of an impoverished orphan named Pip, who comes into a "handsome" fortune at the hands of an anonymous **benefactor**.

The novel begins with a young Pip living with his stern sister and her kind-hearted, blacksmith husband Mr Joe Gargery. Whilst visiting the graves of his parents, Pip encounters a frightening escaped convict, later discovered to be Able Magwitch, who terrifies Pip into helping him. This primary encounter instigates a chain of events that subsequently shape Pip's future.

Pip is then invited by Miss Havisham to visit her estate, Satis House, to play. Miss Havisham is an immensely wealthy, grim lady who lives a peculiar life of seclusion as she is transfixed by the tragic moment of her wedding day, in which she was betrayed by her fiancé.

Here Pip is introduced to Estella, a young, beautiful girl who was adopted by Miss Havisham and raised to be cold and heartless in Miss Havisham's **vicarious** desire to wreak revenge on the male sex. Nonetheless, Pip begins to fall in love with Estella despite her **capricious** and insulting nature.

After visiting Miss Havisham at Satis House over an extensive period of time, Pip receives news that he has come into a "handsome" fortune at the hands of an anonymous benefactor and must depart his **proletarian** upbringing on the marshes to be educated as a gentleman in London.

Driven by his **rapacious** desire to earn Estella's affection and ascend in the 19th century social hierarchy, Pip abandons his honest home life. He becomes ashamed of his origins and instead endeavours to become an affluent and reputable gentleman. However, his insatiable ambition and **burgeoning** arrogance eventually lead to his downfall.

Contrary to his beliefs throughout the entirety of the narrative, Pip discovers that his anonymous "liberal benefactor" had not been Miss Havisham but rather Magwitch, the convict who he had helped at the beginning of the novel. The revelation of his benefactor's identity provokes Pip to confront his own prejudices and biases, realising the power of empathy and forgiveness, as well as understanding that genuine value lies in the integrity of one's character rather than their social status or affluence. As such, Pip comes to possess a newfound appreciation for Joe's unwavering affection and friendship.

Trenchantly: to clearly and forcefully express an opinion.

Benefactor: someone who helps an individual or organisation (monetarily or otherwise).

Vicarious: to feel something through another person's experiences.

Capricious: unpredictable or easily changing.

Proletarian: working class.

Rapacious: greedy; ravenous.

Burgeoning: beginning to grow or flourish.

Camaraderie: a bond of mutual respect and friendship between two people.

When Pip's great expectations eventually send him into debt and perpetual dissatisfaction, he finally realises the genuine value of **camaraderie**, loyalty, and kindness. Pip learns of Estella's suffering under the authority of Miss Havisham and it is revealed that Estella had also learned formative lessons about compassion and love. When reunited, Pip and Estella seek consolation in each other's company.

The novel concludes with a bittersweet yet optimistic inference, as the older version of Pip narrates the story of his life with a newly acquired maturity and wisdom having experienced the tumultuous journey of the expectations and damaging ideals associated with social class.

Section 2
Background Information

Charles Dickens

Charles Dickens was an English writer and social critic whose literary works received unprecedented attention and success during his lifetime. As such, Dickens has earned his place as one of the most successful and talented novelists in the British literary canon.

Dickens was born on the southern coast of England in 1812, growing up during Queen Victoria's reign. He had somewhat of a tumultuous childhood, with his father going to prison for debt, which ended in Dickens leaving school to work in the factories as a young boy. This is widely considered an important event in Dickens's life that had a large impact on his world view. Despite his rough early years, he finished school and went on to work in a number of jobs in law and journalism, eventually being asked to write a serial narrative called *The Pickwick Papers* in 1836. This turned out to be quite a success, and began his literary career. The serialisation of his novels, including the celebrated *Oliver Twist*, became the most popular mode of novel publication in Victorian England.

Creating works such as *Great Expectations*, *A Tale of Two Cities*, and *David Copperfield*, Dickens was highly regarded as one of the greatest, and certainly most popular, novelists of his time. His novels had plenty for all to enjoy and included satire, humour, and his infamous ability to observe and scrutinise society. The common literary themes in Dickens' works have given rise to the term 'Dickensian,' which is used to describe something that parallels his works (e.g. in its reflection of poor social conditions, or comically dislikable characters).

A portrait of Charles Dickens, circa 1860s when Great Expectations was written

19th century England

Society

Set in the early to mid-19th century (to be specific the first chapter of the novel is set in 1812 and the last in 1840), *Great Expectations* provides a meticulous exploration of the societal structures of the early Victorian era.

Industrial Revolution: a time of great advancement of technology with the invention of machinery for manufacturing.

With the **Industrial Revolution** drastically reshaping Western society, the burgeoning ideology of **capitalism** transformed England into a bustling socio-economic sphere in which mass manufacturers of material goods were able to accumulate immense wealth.

Capitalism: a type of economic and political system where trade and industry are privately owned for profit.

Accompanying the emergence of these predominant capitalist ideals, prioritising socio-economic gain above all else, a shift occurred in the hierarchical structure of English society with the emerging presence of the **bourgeoisie** – an affluent, capitalist social class that owned the majority of society's material wealth and means of production at the time. Nonetheless, the class divide between the **proletariat** (the working class) and the bourgeoisie remained significant as the societal superstructure was set out to perpetually validate the rules and ideals of the upper class, enforced through the dominant institutions, such as education, politics, and religion. Essentially, despite the changes brought about by the Industrial Revolution, society was still set out to make the rich richer and the poor poorer. This becomes interesting in the context of *Great Expectations*, as Pip (a working-class boy) inherits a great fortune and rapidly ascends the social hierarchy, demonstrating the benefits and complications of social class mobility in a society that wasn't necessarily **meritocratic**.

Meritocratic: a society in which power and success are given to those who most deserve them.

The rigidity of upper-class life during this period is meticulously portrayed by Dickens throughout *Great Expectations*, displaying the strict social norms that the bourgeoisie were required to adhere to concerning classical education, social etiquette, and physical appearance. In doing so, he also exhibits the stark contrast between the upper-class way of life and that of the lower class in their lack of adhering to these conventions.

George Cruikshank's *The British Beehive* is a perfect visual representation of the socio-economic hierarchy at the time of *Great Expectations*. Not only does it clearly display the levels of wealth and status occupied by different roles and ranks in Victorian society, but also the metaphorical concept of the beehive, that once you are born into your role in society there is little to no logical possibility of ascending or descending in status no matter how hard you work.

The British Beehive by George Cruikshank (drawn circa 1860s)

The metaphor of the beehive also clearly defines the diminishing relationship to physical craft and material production as one ascends. As you can see in the illustration, the occupations defined by physical craftsmanship (e.g. bricklayers, tailors, and bootmakers) are quite low in their hierarchical rank, as opposed to the royal family, who have no relationship to the production of goods or physical labour.

This structure is both proven and problematised by Dickens throughout *Great Expectations* as there is an evident distinction between the proletariat and the bourgeoisie for the majority of the novel. However, Dickens destabilises the notion that you are bound to the status you are born into by showcasing Pip's ascent and descent in the hierarchy and by revealing the low-born origins of Estella, blurring Pip's preconceived idea of the rigidity of this social structure.

Gender

Additionally, during this era the prescribed gender roles of society were just as rigid as the socio-economic hierarchy. Women were bound to their domestic obligations and expected to occupy a kind, nurturing, and maternal role, whereas men were expected to be strong, dominant figures in charge of earning money to support the family unit.

Evidently, across the hierarchical divide, these roles and expectations vary. For example, the working-class man was expected to earn money for his family most commonly via physical labour and craftsmanship, whereas the upper-class gentleman (as seen in the novel) had the increased liberty of investing and gaining capital through less demanding means.

Similarly, the traditional role of the working-class woman was defined by completing physically taxing household chores, whilst the upper-class woman is afforded the liberty of leisure with the help of paid housekeepers.

These rigorously gendered and patriarchally driven ideals of gender at the time of *Great Expectations* are questioned by Dickens through multiple characters in the novel, yet ultimately given that it was originally published in 1861, the extent to which Dickens diverges from these norms doesn't seem overly revolutionary when reading the novel in the 21st century.

Section 3
Chapter-by-Chapter Analysis

Part 1
Chapter 1

Dickens opens *Great Expectations* with an introduction to our protagonist – a young, orphan boy named "Phillip Pirrip," which is shortened to Pip due to his inability to pronounce it in his youth. Through the shortening of his name, seen in the declarative statement "So, I called myself Pip," he is granted his first sense of autonomy over his own identity, tying into the thematic idea of social class Dickens develops further throughout the novel, as names become an important indicator of social class.

Pip's only living relatives are his sister, Mrs Joe Gargery, and her husband the blacksmith. The rest of Pip's family, including his five younger siblings, are buried in a churchyard in a "bleak place surrounded by nettles." It is established that Pip's only memories of his family are the ones he has imagined based on small details on their tombs. Thus, Dickens depicts a harsh, solitudinous life, beset by misery and pain which the narrator refers to as the "universal struggle." From the very first paragraphs of the novel, Dickens characterises proletarian life as one of misery and misfortune, which we will later see juxtaposed against that of the excessive luxury of the upper classes.

Since this text is written in first person, past tense narration, the reader gets the sense that an older, wiser Pip is recounting this tale, which we see in his assertion that his "first most vivid and broad impression of the identity of things seems to me to have been gained on a memorable raw afternoon towards evening." This line starts the tale of the evening that changed the trajectory of Pip's life as he is approached by a terrifying man while he weeps in front of his parents' graves.

The criminal, with "no hat" and "broken shoes" threatens to cut Pip's throat and hauls him upside down to check his pockets. Dickens somewhat foreshadows a significant shift as the criminal enters Pip's life. Not only does he physically turn Pip upside down, but he also **symbolically turns his life upside down in the subsequent procession of the story.**

The description of the criminal, while long, is deliberate in its execution, using **polysyndeton** to emphasise the man's degraded appearance and attitude as he "limped, and shivered, and glared, and growled."

Polysyndeton: sentences that include multiple uses of coordinating conjunctions (and, but, or) in a row for dramatic effect or emphasis.

Similarly, the statement that he "had no hat" might seem a strange description in our modern age; however, in the 1800s hats were associated with status and good gentlemanly conduct, further reinforcing this opening chapter's focus on ideas of social class.

The criminal peppers Pip with hurried questions about his life to ascertain if he is worth threatening for help. Through this, Dickens further portrays the convict's **belligerent nature and low status** in his continuous **monosyllabic exclamations,** "tell us your name!", "quick!", "give it mouth!" His improper use of grammar and highly **colloquial use of language** attests to this low position and lack of education. Dickens emphasises this by using incorrect spelling and omitting letters to enact the cadences and colloquialisms common among the lower classes of this time, seen in phrases such as "Pint out the place!" and "Darn me if I couldn't eat 'em." This establishes the convict's communication with Pip as being purely for survival – saying only what needs to be said, and no more – drastically contrasting the often superfluous **vernacular** of the bourgeoisie characters of the novel. This distinguishes yet another rigid **dichotomy between the wealthy and the impoverished** as the novel progresses.

Colloquial: informal or everyday use of language.

Vernacular: the dialect spoken by a particular group of people.

Dichotomy: a contrast or separation between two things.

The criminal threatens Pip again and asks him to fetch a "file" (a tool to break the chains on his leg) and "wittles" (food to eat) and bring them back the next morning which Pip agrees to out of fear.

The clear characterisation of Pip in this opening chapter plays into the ideas Dickens purports throughout the novel around identity and ambition, or more specifically of inherited identity and self-made identity. At the time of writing, it was very much accepted that a working-class individual was unlikely to progress in society beyond what he was born to. Thus, characterising Pip initially as proletariat sets certain expectations in the mind of the audience, which Dickens later challenges throughout the novel. Consequently, he is also able to highlight the difficulties Pip experiences around his identity as he moves through social hierarchies. But for now, he is a young, inexperienced, and naïve child who has struggled much in life, the identity of his familial life only available to him in his imagination.

Chapter 2

Pip hurries from the graveyard to his home at the blacksmiths where we are introduced to Mrs Joe Gargery and her husband Joe. Mrs Joe Gargery is characterised as a mean and angry woman with a keen hand for punishment as she brings out the "Tickler," a piece of cane she uses to punish Pip and Joe. Contrarily, Joe is characterised as "good-natured," "sweet-tempered," and "easy-going."

This juxtaposition between the two is further depicted by Dickens in their **diametrically** opposing physical attributes. While Joe is illustrated as a "fair man, with curls of flaxen hair on each side of his smooth face," giving a sense of innocence and naïvety, Mrs Joe is characterised as having "black hair and eyes, [and] a prevailing redness of skin." In this way, Dickens places a hyperbolic focus on the physical attributes of characters as a means of outwardly portraying their personalities and inner attributes.

Diametrically: completely (when referencing opposition).

Mrs Joe is in a rage as she has been out looking for Pip. There is a sense of camaraderie between Pip and Joe as they conspiratorially share their fears of the woman, and their relationship is shown to be selfless and righteous. Throughout the novel, this camaraderie is further established to be intrinsically wedded to the honourable, satisfying, and tangible life of the working class, inevitably becoming distorted with Pip's hierarchical ambitions. Therefore, their current relationship is seen as authentic and **filial**, one that is untarnished by the materialistic views of Victorian society which will be revealed in the coming chapters.

Filial: relating to a son or daughter.

We also see in this chapter the first instances of Pip grappling with morality, where he has "guilty knowledge" of what he is about to do. As he gets up in the early hours of the morning to steal food for the convict, he hears every creak of the house yelling at him: "Stop thief!" This not only shows his juvenile innocence, yet also signifies the authentic moral righteousness which Pip – as a child and proletarian figure – embodies prior to his introduction to the calculated and economical ethics of the bourgeoisie. However, his fear of the criminal wins out and he steals some food from the pantry and a file from the forge and heads out into the misty marshes.

Chapter 3

Pip heads into the miserable morning to find the convict. At first, he comes across another convict who "was everything that the other man was; except that he had not the same face." Pip thinks that it's the convict's companion, the young man who was threatened to be worse even than the first convict. However, the man runs away and Pip continues on to meet the convict.

Pip delivers the food to the convict who eats ravenously. Dickens viscerally describes the convict "gobbling mincemeat," taking "strong sharp sudden bites," and making "a chop at the jaws," which demonstrates his low social class through the complete disregard for gentlemanly etiquette. He is instinctually driven by a canine hunger, eating purely as an act of survival, which even Pip looks down upon, equating the convict to a "large dog" eating his food.

Dickens also continues the use of incorrect spelling and grammar to articulate the convict's lack of education and low-class status, which is an important point of analysis when discussing the correlation between social status and education.

> **KEY POINT :**
> These scenes (and quotes) are important to note when distinguishing between the lifestyles and behaviours of characters at each end of the social hierarchy. A recurring theme that Dickens returns to is this concept: that **there is always someone both higher and lower in the hierarchy than Pip** – somewhere to aspire to or look down on.

Chapter 4

Pip returns home, with a guilty conscience, to find Mrs Joe readying the house for Christmas Day guests by putting up "clean white curtains" and cooking a feast of pork, greens, and "a pair of stuffed fowl." This scene immediately juxtaposes Pip leaving the cold and ravenous convict, allowing Dickens to both depict the large gap between the lowest class and the working class as well as establish an incongruence between the everyday lives of the Gargerys and the extensive arrangements needed to contrive a more upper-class appearance in the company of guests.

Joe's discomfort in his ill-fitting holiday clothes attest to how this performative guise of middle-class gentility creates discomfort. This idea is furthered by the metaphor of Joe's abrasive clothing seeming to "graze" his body. This highlights Joe's genuine moral righteousness, being uncomfortable with the pressure to arbitrarily conform to the appearance of the upper classes.

As the guests convene around the dining table, an overt hierarchy is established between the esteemed guests and Pip who is "squeezed in at an acute angle of the tablecloth" and "regaled with the scaly tips of the drumsticks and fowls." Pip is then harangued by the guests who think him unappreciative. They equate him to a pig and lecture him on the ungrateful nature of youth. There is a sense in these paragraphs that Dickens ridicules the middle classes' need to attain moral superiority over a child.

Dickens' detest of the performative and hypocritical nature of the middle class is further explored in the juxtaposition between the guests and Joe. Mr Wopsle, the church clerk, says grace in a dramatic and insincere way, whereas Joe gives Pip extra gravy from his own plate. The guests' gratitude is a mere theatrical display, completely disingenuous; however, Joe displays true humility as he selflessly offers food to Pip. This juxtaposition highlights the issues with the **performative moral righteousness of the middle class** as they only display a theatrical façade of genuine ethics, all of which is bred by the desire for social superiority.

As the dining proceeds Mrs Joe goes to retrieve the pork pie – which Pip had given to the convict – making Pip's guilt swell until he "could bear no more" and "ran for [his] life." However, he only reaches the door before being met by a "party of soldiers with their muskets."

Chapter 5

Pip, startled by the impending doom of the soldiers, soon finds out, to his relief, that they are not there for him but to have some irons (handcuffs) mended by the blacksmith. He is even momentarily saved from the discovery of the missing pie and Mrs Joe's impending wrath. In fact, the coming of the soldiers and the excitement of the search for the escaped fugitives seems to put everyone in a good mood, with Mr Pumblechook handing out wine liberally.

Pip notes that the suffering of the convicts is "a terrible good sauce for a dinner," indicating how the guests are using the convict's misfortune as a source of amusement and entertainment, rather than seeing the sombre reality of the cold and hungry men who will likely be hanged for their crimes. Through this, Dickens indicates that the guests view the convicts as less than human, their capture a mere sport to liven their Christmas dinner, which along with earlier animalistic descriptions of the convicts, depict those of the lowest classes as barely worth considering with human decency.

The soldiers, Mr Wopsle, Joe, and Pip are then tasked with searching for these convicts. After searching the marshes, they come upon the two convicts fighting in the mud, shouting "murder" and "convicts." They are consequently arrested but Pip's convict makes an admission before they take him away. He announces that he was the one to steal the pie and file from the blacksmith's establishment, effectively freeing Pip from any suspicion. This shows the morality of the convict, who had no reason to do such a thing other than to repay Pip for his kindness.

Throughout these scenes, Dickens explores the nuances of morality across classes, showing the guests' exhilarated attitudes to the search for the struggling convicts, which is contrasted with Joe's view of the convicts as "poor miserable fellow-creature[s]" and the convict's selfless admission to Pip's crime. Thus, the acceptance of the simple, proletariat life is depicted as one of morality.

Chapter 6

After the prisoners are taken away, Joe carries Pip home while Pip internally expresses his guilt about not telling Joe "the whole truth" of his interactions with the convict, demonstrating a genuine display of morality. Once home, the guests try to determine how the convict entered and Pip, exhausted, is hauled upstairs to bed by Mrs Joe. Pip recalls how his guilt lasted long after the family stopped bothering to talk about the adventure, demonstrating the lasting integrity of Pip's morality over the passing fancies of the entertainment of the middle class. This is a very short chapter which mostly expresses Pip's guilt for not telling Joe about the convict and furthers his child-like identity.

Chapter 7

This chapter begins with Pip reflecting on his educational upbringing; from barely making out the words on his family's tombstones to his rather lacking education by Mr Wopsle's great-aunt. These former experiences attest to the lack of conventional learning granted to working-class children, quite in contrast to his experiences of education later in the novel.

However, through Pip's dismal schooling, Dickens alludes to Pip's burgeoning aspirations for self-improvement as he "struggle[s] through the alphabet as if it had been a bramble-bush," eventually beginning "in a purblind groping way, to read, write, and cipher." This is our first glimpse of Pip as one who **blurs the boundaries of class through ambition and hard work.**

Back in the current moment, Pip shows a poorly written message to Joe, who can read even less than Pip, and Joe tells Pip that teaching him will have to be done in secret, away from Mrs Joe. This begins a heart-warming conversation between the two, with Joe expressing how he had been the one to insist Pip stayed at the house despite Pip's mean attitude as a boy. He also expresses that he wished Pip didn't have to be punished with the cane and that he "could take it all on [himself]." Joe, then, is characterised as someone who always sees the good in everyone – even Mrs Joe, calling her a "master-mind." Thus, accepting and finding joy in the proletariat life is characterised as a moral and just pursuit.

This is contrasted with Mrs Joe upon her return home. She brings news that a reclusive, rich, and important upper-class woman has invited Pip to her home to play and thus she must make Pip presentable. She does this by scrubbing him raw and putting him in "clean linen of the stiffest character," which is reminiscent of Joe's earlier discomfort in his fine clothes at Christmas. Mrs Joe's yearning for hierarchical gain and her subsequent insecurity in Pip's working-class appearance – as he is "grimed with crock and dirt" – is shown in the thorough process in which Pip is cleaned to attain a level of cleanliness appropriate for upper-class company.

Dickens ends the chapter by foreshadowing the drastic changes that will occur to Pip's life following this invitation. He does this through the uncertainty with which Pip approaches the process, not knowing "why on earth I was going to play at Miss Havisham's and what on earth I was expected to play at."

Chapter 8

The following day, Mr Pumblechook takes Pip to Miss Havisham's gloomy estate where he meets a young woman named Estella. Within moments of meeting Pip, Estella neglects to refer to him by name, which Dickens had established in the very first chapter to be a fundamental piece of Pip's identity. Instead, Estella's references to Pip as "boy" suggest an immediate sense of disdain held by the upper-class Estella towards the proletarian Pip.

As they enter, Satis House is seen by Pip as a dark and gloomy place with "no glimpse of daylight," which is starkly contrasted against the warm home he shares with Joe. This instils a sense of unfamiliarity, like a threshold between Pip's current experience and that of the upper class which is shrouded with uncertainty. As they walk, the name Satis is translated by Estella to mean "enough house," which ironically alludes to the consuming greed of the bourgeoisie who are never truly satisfied.

Estella leaves Pip with Miss Havisham, a very strange lady surrounded by wedding finery that has withered and yellowed over the years, just as she "had withered like the dress." Through this unsettling bridal imagery, Dickens makes Miss Havisham's physical appearance a prominent feature of her secluded existence as an upper-class woman.

Through her appearance, Dickens may also be alluding to the ravages of upper-class society on an individual over time and the idea that having everything does not necessarily lead to a happy and fulfilled life. We can see this in Pip's earlier conversations with Joe, who despite having had an abusive upbringing and a simple life, is still overwhelmingly positive, loving, and full of life. Miss Havisham, on the other hand, is likened to a "skeleton [that] seemed to have dark eyes that moved and looked at me."

Not only does Pip recognise the lack of life present in Miss Havisham's room, but he also notices "that her watch had stopped at twenty minutes to nine, and that a clock in her room had stopped at twenty to nine," introducing the prominent theme of time (or the neglect of time) that persists throughout the entirety of the novel. There is a stark divide between the working class, who heavily rely on the temporal marker of time to dictate their lives and their labour, and the upper class who are afforded the privilege of ignoring the restrictions of time itself. This is epitomised in Miss Havisham's capacity to "transfix" time. This notion becomes particularly prominent is Miss Havisham's statement "I know nothing of the days of the week; I know nothing of the weeks of the year."

Miss Havisham then asks Pip to play with Estella and they play cards. Through Miss Havisham's "sick fantasy" to see Pip play, Dickens emphasises how she is afforded the luxury to spend her time indulging in the manipulation of Pip without worrying about the constraints of practical life. It also alludes to the authority of the upper class, who can, at a whim, influence and control the lower classes in a way that is morally **unconscionable**. Thus, from the outset of Miss Havisham's introduction, **she is characterised as affluent yet morally corrupt, using a young boy to fulfil her fantasies.**

Unconscionable: unethical or immoral.

The two play and Estella continues to insult Pip, commenting on his shoes, clothes, and language. This begins Pip's assessment of his own place in the social hierarchy; thoughts he had not considered before due to his simple upbringing. Multiple times throughout the chapter, and in its concluding lines, Pip remembers Estella's **reproach**. He obsesses over the fact he is "a common labouring-boy; that [his] hands were coarse; that [his] boots were thick; that [he] had fallen into a despicable habit of calling knaves Jacks; that [he] was much more ignorant than [he] had considered [himself] last night, and generally that [he] was in a low-lived bad way." We can see again here the extended use of polysyndeton, which serves to emphasise the **disparaging** way which Pip is talking to himself after only one interaction with upper-class society.

Reproach: to reprimand or express disapproval.

Disparage: to see something as worth nothing.

Genteel: to be refined and respectable, often associated with a high social status.

Furthermore, Pip belittles and speaks badly about Joe, resenting the fact he had not been "more **genteelly** brought up." Therefore, Dickens delineates a shift in Pip's previous camaraderie with Joe, as his views begin to be warped by the morally contentious values of the bourgeoisie. Pip is then fed and told to come back in six days. Dickens' recurring symbol of the lower class having a dog-like status once again surfaces as Pip is further dehumanised by Estella putting "bread and meat down on the stones of the yard" for him to eat. This continues to demonstrate that those lower on the social hierarchy are perceived as animalistic figures devoid of human value. Pip then heads home, distraught with his identity and supposed shortcomings.

Chapter 9

On arriving home, Pip is confronted by Mrs Joe and Mr Pumblechook who desperately want to know what happened at the Havisham estate. However, Pip lies to them as he isn't able to describe what he saw, nor could he speak of Miss Havisham in a way that others could understand. Interestingly, unlike his initial guilty conscience when lying about his interactions with the convict in chapter 1, Pip feels no guilt in lying to Mrs Joe and Mr Pumblechook, starting his decline into dubious morality. He tells them of the array of "marvels," being "handed cake and wine at the coach-window," and having "played with flags" and swords. However, when Joe enters and is amazed by his outrageous stories, Pip is "overtaken by penitence" in not immediately telling the truth to Joe.

Pip escapes Mrs Joe and goes to Joe's forge to tell him everything. Joe admonishes his behaviour, morally stating that "lies is lies" and that lying is no way to move out of their low-born status. Joe innocently advises Pip that the hierarchical ascension he desires should only be achieved through honest meritocratic work. Pip accepts and respects this advice from Joe, although thoughts of Joe's common status and dress are still in his mind. At the conclusion of the chapter, Pip thinks about how Mrs Joe and Joe sitting in the kitchen is a lowly position and Miss Havisham probably had never even been in her own kitchen, which is a place for servants. Thus, the initial imagery of the kitchen setting as a warm and comforting place is starting to be warped by Pip's sudden unhappiness with his social status.

Chapter 10

Since Pip's trip to Satis House, he has renewed energy to continue his learning and become "uncommon," so he encourages Biddy, the shopkeeper at Mr Wopsle's great-aunt's shop, to help him with his studies. However, Pip can now see the gap in his schooling that he couldn't see before going to Satis House, commenting that it "would take time to become uncommon, under these circumstances."

Pip then heads to the bar at the Three Jolly Bargemen to retrieve Joe where he has an encounter with a strange man talking with Joe and Mr Wopsle. The man makes a point to stir his drink with a file, suspiciously similar to the one Pip had given the convict earlier in the novel. This startles Pip and brings his guilty conscience to the fore. The man then gives a small sum of money to Pip which foreshadows the later fortune Pip will receive from an anonymous benefactor who is eventually revealed as the convict from the beginning of the novel.

Through these scenes, Dickens cleverly reminds the reader of the seemingly unimportant occurrences at the beginning of the novel which will later become pivotal to the narrative. Pip isn't overjoyed at the money at all, and only sees it as a source of his guilt which he still harbours for helping the convict all those years ago.

Chapter 11

Pip returns for his visit at Satis House. He encounters a group of visitors, "three ladies and one gentleman," all deemed to be "toadies and humbugs" and he is once again confronted with the dark, timeless, atmosphere of Miss Havisham's estate.

Instead of playing cards, Miss Havisham commands Pip to enter an equally unsettling room in which "daylight was completely excluded, [with] an airless smell that was oppressive." In the centre of the room was "a long table with a tablecloth spread on it, as if a feast had been in preparation when the house and the clocks all stopped together." The table was adorned with a centrepiece revealed by Miss Havisham to have been her own "bride-cake" which was now covered in cobwebs. Through this continual warped marital imagery, Dickens obscures the conventional upper-class ideals of marriage and the bride, portraying the festering arrangements of a wedding in which the bride is left to decompose with her surroundings. A sense of morbidity is also evoked by her statement that this table "is where I will be laid when I am dead. They shall come and look at me." Not only does this grotesque imagery elicit a sense of discomfort, it also epitomises Miss Havisham's destiny as an ageing, unmarried woman of the bourgeoisie, inevitably meeting her fate as an inanimate display of wealth, to be objectified and observed.

The audience is now starting to get a sense of the reasons for Miss Havisham's behaviour, including why Pip was invited to play in the first place. As a woman scorned on her wedding day, Miss Havisham has brought up the beautiful Estella to hurt men as they had hurt her, with Pip being the first test subject. This is solidified in the following chapter when Miss Havisham says, "break their hearts my pride and hope, break their hearts and have no mercy!"

Pip is tasked with walking Miss Havisham around the grotesque bride table, as if imitating the walk she might have done as a bride. The guests Pip had encountered earlier enter the room as they are walking and it is revealed they are there for her birthday. However, she strictly expresses "I don't suffer it to be spoken of" once again attesting to the disparaging attitudes of Victorian society towards ageing women as well as her own negligence to the societal regulations of time itself.

Pip and Estella then play cards again before he is sent to the yard to eat like a dog. It is here that Pip encounters "a pale young gentleman with red eyelids and light hair." This boy, later revealed as Herbert Pocket, challenges Pip to fight for no reason. Through their employment of the "laws of the game!" and the "regular rules!" of a gentlemanly fight, Dickens suggests that Pip and the newly acquainted Herbert are somewhat imitating the customs of the upper-class gentlemen of whom they desire to become. More so, the rules and the fight itself are seen to be a futile display of juvenile play, akin to the futility of the rules and etiquette of the bourgeoisie.

After the fight, Estella commands Pip to come and kiss her, taunting him with a fleeting moment of affection. This aligns with Miss Havisham's manipulative demands for Estella to "break their hearts and have no mercy," endeavouring to vicariously seek revenge towards men through Estella's relationship with Pip – a notion further elucidated as the narrative progresses.

Chapter 12

The next chapter occurs over a span of months in which Pip visits Miss Havisham every other day to push her around the room in a wheeled garden chair. On one occasion he is asked by Miss Havisham to sing and Pip recalls the song "Old Clem," an iron-working song Joe often hummed at the forge. Emphasised by the heavy use of consonance in its lyrics "with a clink for the stout – Old Clem! Beat it out, beat it out Old Clem!", the song symbolises the spiritual and joyous unity of Joe and his physical craftsmanship as a blacksmith. However, when Miss Havisham and Estella join in "in a low brooding voice," the jovial nature of the song is completely subverted. Instead, it becomes a "subdued" lull when detached from the working class and unnaturally forced into an upper-class environment, sung by Miss Havisham and Estella who have no attachments to the gratification of physical labour.

As the chapter progresses, Dickens illuminates a **shift in Pip's relationship with Joe.** Rather than confiding in Joe, Pip begins to rely on his "complete confidence in no one but Biddy" from whom he can gain knowledge, **aiding him in his aspirations for class ascension.** As such, Dickens suggests a shift in Pip's priorities, diverting from his morally honest relationship with Joe to a somewhat self-serving relationship with Biddy, **prioritising his desire to be a gentleman over genuine human connection.**

Biddy says that she has "a deep concern [for] everything [he] told her" about his time with Miss Havisham, which foreshadows the insidious future Pip has in store as he grapples to move into a higher social class. The chapter closes with Miss Havisham asking Pip of his arrangements to be "apprenticed" to Joe. She takes matters into her own hands, exercising her autonomy by deciding that Pip is old enough to be apprenticed to Joe immediately. She invites Joe to Satis House to receive the "premiums" earned by Pip from his visits. Upon learning that Joe is invited to Satis House, Mrs Joe goes on a "rampage" again, showing how desperately she wants acknowledgement for her efforts to appear of a higher class and how deeply unhappy she is in her current low-class status.

Throughout this chapter it is clear **Pip is going through several shifts in his character.** His growing attachment to Estella, encouraged by Miss Havisham, **completely change his relationship with Joe, his morality, and his own self-confidence.** Not only does he not tell the truth and disregard Joe but he becomes obsessed with impressing Estella through the overwhelming influence of Miss Havisham in those "misty yellow rooms."

Chapter 13

Joe dresses in his finest clothes and heads with Pip to Satis House. Through Joe's venture into Miss Havisham's estate, Dickens directly juxtaposes the seemingly inadequate proletariat to the esteemed upper class. Illustrated to be "dreadfully uncomfortable" and out of place whilst once again donning his "Sunday clothes," Joe serves as an embodiment of this working-class figure. As such, when entering Satis House, Joe's discomfort and subsequently the shame Pip feels to be associated with Joe, demonstrates this **undeniable shift in Pip's morality.** Pip values Miss Havisham's perceptions of himself and Joe above his previously **immutable** filial relationship with Joe.

Immutable: not changing.

Miss Havisham rewards Pip for his visits with a payment of twenty five guineas. When Pip and Joe return home, Mrs. Joe is impressed by the amount and Pumblechook takes credit for Pip's success, though Pip sees through his hypocrisy and self-interest.

Chapter 14

Pip continues to feel ashamed of his home life as Dickens elicits a diminished sense of magic and admiration felt by Pip in relation to his home and previously unwavering aspirations to "go into the forge" and be apprenticed to Joe. Dickens articulates this through Pip's changed perspective from being an innocent child, viewing the "parlour as a most elegant saloon" and "the forge as the glowing road to manhood and independence," to now in his adolescence perceiving his working-class life to be "coarse and common." The harsh **alliteration** of "course and common" is indicative of the jarring finality of Pip's shift in perspective.

Alliteration: repetition of a sound at the beginning of closely connected words.

Thoughts of Miss Havisham and Estella continue to penetrate Pip's thoughts whilst working as a blacksmith, further exemplifying Pip's embarrassment in his lowly job. Pip desires to see Estella again, yet dreads that she might see him whilst looking his "grimiest and commonest." Throughout this chapter Pip's altered sense of identity resulting from his burgeoning ambition for class ascension is highlighted. This is solidified by Dickens when Pip admits that "the change was made in me; the thing was done." He acknowledges that a great shift had occurred in his life, the beginnings of his great expectations.

Chapter 15

This chapter begins with Pip's ambition to learn all that he can to escape his "deficient" home life. Through Pip's constant drive to find any information he can with what little he has, Dickens further establishes the themes of **ambition** and **social class.** At this point in the novel, Pip believes that education and ambition alone can see him ascend in the social hierarchy. Yet, the author later questions this notion as Pip's only real way to ascend is through his inherited fortune. Thus, Dickens is setting the stage to reveal the true inequalities within the class system.

Pip attempts to teach Joe everything he has learned from Biddy and others. He does this not just to help Joe, but to remove some of the shame Pip feels at Joe's lack of education. However, Dickens reiterates that Joe is satisfied with his social class, as he seems to be there only to please Pip and not to increase his own social standing. Pip, on the other hand, is fuelled by his longing of Estella who he is reminded of by everything he looks at. Miss Havisham has succeeded in her goal to make Pip infatuated with Estella, as Pip looks for any excuse to go to her, pleading with Joe for a half day off to go to Satis House.

Journeyman: a worker of a learned trade who is employed after completing an apprenticeship.

Dolge Orlick is then introduced as the **journeyman** at the forge. He is described as a "morose [...] broad shouldered loose-limbed swarthy fellow of great strength." Here Dickens uses **asyndeton** to place emphasis on Orlick's physical characteristics, which are employed to garner an insight into his personality (this is something the author does throughout the novel as we've seen with Miss Havisham, Mrs Joe, and Joe). Both his unsettling name and somewhat grotesque and villainous physical appearance elicit a devious sense of mistrust in the reader, further evinced in his argument with Mrs Joe and consequently his physical fight with Joe.

Asyndeton: literary technique which omits the conjunctions between words to create speed, emphasis, or urgency in the sentence.

The fight is provoked by his suspicion that Pip will take his job at the forge as Joe had allowed Pip to have a "half-holiday" which Orlick believes to be unfair treatment. When the fight is over, Orlick is left with a few bruises but the pair make up and share a beer before Pip heads to Miss Havisham's house. This fight is in stark contrast with Pip's earlier fight with the young gentleman at Satis House. Pip's fight had no sensible reasoning, nor was there a sense of camaraderie or mutual understanding after the fight like Joe extended to Orlick. This furthers the reader's perception of the **hollow morality of the upper class.**

Upon visiting Satis House without invitation in the hope of seeing Estella, Miss Havisham informs Pip that Estella is "abroad, [...] educating for a lady; far out of reach; prettier than ever; admired by all who see her." As such, through Miss Havisham's persistent proclamations of Estella's beauty, and thus her corruption of Pip's desires, Dickens further confirms Miss Havisham's self-indulgent "malignant enjoyment" in manipulating Pip, **vicariously utilising Estella's physical beauty as an instrument with which she aspires to exact revenge on men.** Pip then joins Mr Wopsle and Mr Pumblechook for an "intellectual evening" before discovering that Mrs Joe had been attacked in their home.

Chapter 16

Details of the attack emerge as they come upon the scene of the beaten Mrs Joe. She is gravely injured after being hit with something "blunt and heavy" on her head and spine. There is a "convict's leg-iron" lying close to her body which is assumed to be the weapon. Pip notes that it had been "filed **asunder**" just like the convict's cuffs in the first chapter. Pip feels a great guilt at seeing the shackles which might have come from the convict he helped long ago; however, he is not so naïve to believe that the convict was at fault and deduces that either Orlick or the man at the bar with the file were responsible for the attack. This version of Pip is much changed from the beginning of the novel when he was gullible and uneducated; hence, Dickens depicts the maturity he has gained in pursuing education. His guilt also intimates that Pip's morality has not been completely lost in his pursuit for class ascension.

Asunder: something in separate pieces.

Following the attack, Mrs Joe is greatly incapacitated and can only 'talk' by writing on a slate with the help of Pip. However, Pip admits that despite the horrific nature of her incident "her temper was greatly improved, and she was patient." This demonstrates a shift in Pip's familial life. He is no longer governed by the "coarse" hand of Mrs Joe. Thus, **the attack and its aftermath are symbolic of Pip's maturation.**

Biddy joins their household to help look after Mrs Joe and she helps Pip figure out what Mrs Joe means when she repeatedly traces a "curious T" on her slate. Biddy deciphers that Mrs Joe's "mysterious sign" was an incriminating reference to Orlick and his hammer, who Pip suspects is the attacker despite Mrs Joe's affectionate attitude towards the man.

Chapter 17

Pip's shift in maturity is increasingly obvious in this chapter as he starts to see Biddy as a potential love interest. Biddy is used by Dickens to contrast Estella. Biddy's kindness and common good looks are diametrically opposed with Estella's beauty and mean attitude. Through this contrast, Dickens begins to establish the internal conflict experienced by Pip throughout chapters 17–19.

Pip wishes that he could be content with the honesty and merit of his working-class life. He knows his desires "to be so very mad and misplaced," yet he is unable to suppress or deny his intrinsic ambition and "hunger" to ascend the social hierarchy in pursuit of Estella. Ultimately, Dickens makes clear **Pip's major character flaw, that of his ambition.**

Pip confides in Biddy, confessing "I want to be a gentleman" and admitting his dissatisfaction with his current life on the forge. He overtly expresses his thoughts that if he was not so captivated by Estella he could have a satisfying life with Biddy; however, through their conversation, Dickens also emphasises Pip's emerging arrogance. He views himself as superior to Biddy, having "got beyond her" in knowledge and education, deeming himself to have greater life aspirations. Thus, **Dickens suggests that the desperate pursuit for hierarchical ascension makes one egotistical and abandon familial connections for hollow goals.**

Pip's internal conflict progresses as he contemplates his lack of gratitude towards Biddy for her efforts in educating him and considers whether he could make a more "natural" and "wholesome" life for himself if he was to marry Biddy. He explicitly articulates this when he says: "If I could only get myself to fall in love with you [...] *that* would be the thing for me." However, both Pip and Biddy know that this will never happen as Pip will never be satisfied, which spurs his constant confusion.

While he knows that "Biddy was immeasurably better than Estella, and that the plain honest working life to which [he] was born, had nothing in it to be ashamed of, but offered [him] sufficient means of self-respect and happiness" he cannot let go of his dreams of self-improvement. Miss Havisham and the very distant possibility of a wealthy, upper-class life thwart his attempts to be at peace with what he has.

Through this, Dickens demonstrates the true **duality of Pip's intentions,** where on one hand he is deeply dissatisfied with his working-class life and yearns to become a gentleman worthy of Estella's praise and attention, yet on the other hand he acknowledges the genuine satisfaction derived from honest human connections and the gratifying physical craftsmanship which he currently practises.

Chapter 18

Four months of Pip's apprenticeship have passed, and he is sat at the Jolly Bargeman listening to Mr Wopsle regale the tale of a murder in London with excessive dramatics when a lawyer introduces himself as Mr Jaggers. He does so with arrogance and speaks with Mr Wopsle in such a way as to make him look stupid to all those gathered. His behaviour is typical of high-class characters in the novel, so the audience gets the sense that he is also of a higher class and thus looking down on those in the Jolly Bargeman. He announces that he is there to see Pip and Joe, so they head back to their home to talk. Pip recognises the man from Miss Havisham's house and already has expectations for the nature of his visit.

Mr Jaggers uses legal **jargon** and scripted formal dialogue throughout the chapter. His repeated exchanges with Joe and Pip, such as "I express no opinions" or "I am paid for my services, or I shouldn't render them" exemplifies the **emotionally detached, meretricious nature of upper-class conversations.** In expressing this, Dickens associates the bourgeoisie legal system, and consequently the educated upper classes, with the **prioritisation of financial gain over authenticity in human relationships.** Although expressed in a different way, this is exactly the same process Pip has been going through since his first visit to Satis House and is synonymous with the bourgeoisie lifestyle.

Jargon: technical language used by a specific profession.

Meretricious: something that is outwardly showy but cheap in reality.

The self-proclaimed "pretty well known" lawyer relays that he has been told to tell Joe that Pip "will come into a handsome property" and "great expectations." This is an incredibly significant moment in Pip's life and the second major turning point in the novel.

Continuing to employ his calculated, upper-class vernacular, Mr Jaggers proceeds to explain that the anonymous benefactor wants Pip to "be brought up as a gentleman" but with two conditions: Pip must keep his name, and the identity of his benefactor must remain a secret. By this point, Pip arrogantly assumes that Miss Havisham must be the benefactor so that he would one day become a gentleman and marry Estella. Yet, with the hindsight of the novel's denouement (as well as the narrator's hindsight as an older version of Pip) this is understood to be a false assumption.

In becoming aware of his "great expectations" and fortune, Pip begins to value economic gain over genuine relationships when he accepts the lawyer's contractual guardianship over his own emotional connection with Joe. Through the alliteration and **plosive** sounds in Mr Jaggers' speech informing Pip of his expectations, **Dickens hyperbolises the reduction of relationships to purely transactional exchanges under the influence of the upper echelons of society.**

Plosive: a consonant which stops the airflow out of the mouth such as *p, k, t, d, g,* and *b*.

Pip has minimal dialogue during this interaction, and the dialogue he does have is typically interrupted by Mr Jaggers. This alludes to his lack of power in this exchange, contributing to his alienation and objectification under the guidance of the economically and educationally superior Mr Jaggers, showing the capitalistic nature of money enabling power and intellect.

In contrast to Pip's agreement with Jaggers, Joe rejects the condescending offer for monetary compensation for the loss of Pip's services at the forge. Instead, he states that money cannot compensate for the loss of Pip, his best friend. This shows that although Joe is treated like the "village idiot," he has knowledge that Pip is far from discovering, that of **the importance of human connection and affection.** This demonstrates Joe's valuing of his camaraderie with Pip over a transactional exchange from which he would economically benefit.

Thus, through Joe, **Dickens condemns the superficial ethics of the bourgeoisie that favour financial superiority over "amiable honest-hearted" empathy**.

Chapter 19

Following the reception of his "great expectations," Pip's perceptions become even more pervaded by bourgeoisie ideals. Articulated in his blatantly arrogant feelings of "condescension" of everyone in the village that infiltrate his once optimistic and infantile admiration of his home. His arrogance is further extrapolated in the **personification** of the cattle that had once accused him of his guilt in the opening chapters of the novel, but now they "stare as long as possible at the possessor of such great expectations."

Personification: to give human characteristics to something non-human.

At this point in the novel, Pip is ignorant to the genuine fulfilment achieved by Joe in his honest trade, instead being further enveloped into the bourgeoisie mentality of valuing money over human connection, such as when he aspires to one day "remove Joe into a higher sphere" to escape the shame of working-class life. Similarly, when Biddy explains Joe's contentment with his life, Pip arrogantly assumes she is jealous of his new-found wealth. However, we see through the narration from the mature Pip that he is self-aware of his "virtuous and superior" adolescent mentality indicating a future character development.

Venturing into town with the benefits of his newly received "fortune," Pip experiences the stark contrast between the treatment granted to those with money and those without, realising the "stupendous power of money." This is exemplified in Pip's experience with Mr Trabb the tailor, a "prosperous old bachelor" who is at first inhospitable but then instantly flocks to "congratulate" Pip and offer him exceptional, attentive service when hearing of his "rise in fortune" and recently acquired "handsome property." Through this, Dickens demonstrates the overt shifts in the attitudes of the upper class when interacting with those of lower or higher socio-economic status to themselves.

His treatment of Pip is also directly juxtaposed with his barking commands to his young assistant, such as "give me number four, you!" This illuminates the prevailing notion of the bourgeoisie abusing their social and economic superiority in exploiting those of a lower hierarchical position. Also, by using the second-person pronoun "you" instead of the assistant's name, Mr Trabb is dehumanising his assistant in much the same way Estella did when referring to Pip as "boy" earlier in the novel. Names are used by Dickens as important **tools for establishing social class, respect, and identity across the novel.**

Pip's relationship with Mr Pumblechook also changes with his sudden fortune. Pumblechook's regular condescension and lecturing towards Pip is replaced by a theatrical expression of camaraderie, referring to Pip as a "dear young friend" and offering him "wine" and an abundance of indulgences.

When the time finally comes for Pip to depart home, his internal conflict remerges. Throughout the chapter Pip is often depicted alone, having lonely nights due to his snobbish attitude. Yet when he's leaving he feels remorse, considering heading back to the house to do a better farewell and shedding tears for his life in the village. However, he is indecisive and doesn't turn back, instead seeing the mists parting as if the "world lay spread before [him]," a metaphor for his great expectations. **Dickens uses the imagery of the village to show the beginning of Pip's new life and rise in circumstances.** When he is younger, Pip describes his home as dreary marshes yet when he is leaving the village is quiet with "light mists."

Part 2

Chapter 20

Pip parts from his rural life on the marshes and is engulfed into the bustling yet "dismal [...] metropolis" of London. Dickens articulates Pip's feelings of inundation through an abundance of vivid imagery, with "dilapidated" buildings and "crooked, narrow and dirty" streets pervaded by "hot exhausted air, and by the dust and grit that lay thick on everything." He also notices the imposing, **poignant** smells of "spirits and beer" and the general urban atmosphere. The city itself becomes somewhat personified, serving not only as a backdrop to Pip's journey of class ascension but also an imposing force that influences Pip throughout the novel, fostering and reflecting the tarnished, polluted moral virtues of the economically driven bourgeoisie.

Poignant: a pungent smell.

Arriving in London, Pip is further acquainted with the lawyer, Mr Jaggers, and is made aware of his powerful status and influence, as it is not just Pip, but "other people" gathering outside Jaggers' office waiting to be spoken to. These diverse crowds of people are denoted by Pip as "testimonies to the popularity" of his guardian, provoking a further admiration towards the lawyer on Pip's behalf. However, despite Jaggers' importance, his space, much like Miss Havisham's, is described with imagery of death and decay. He has an "old, rusty pistol" and his chair of "deadly black horsehair" is described as "like a coffin."

Chapter 21

Pip is introduced to Wemmick who takes him to his lodgings at Barnard's Inn. Wemmick is described as "the clerk in the next room" to Jaggers' whose "dry" and "mechanical" demeanour whilst occupied by his work contrasts greatly to his **genial** joyousness and optimism in his personal life, separate from work.

Genial: pleasant and friendly.

In prior chapters Dickens has set up London as a depraved city; however, we now see Pip being further introduced to London's darker side in his conversation with Wemmick. Pip asks about London's devious nature, to which Wemmick replies that you will get robbed or murdered there same as anywhere else. When Pip tries to "soften" this by saying that those things would only happen to you if you had made an enemy, Wemmick disagrees saying "there's not much bad blood about. They'll do it, if there's anything to be got by it." This insinuates that London is a place where people put their goals above all else. Thus, Dickens further establishes the cut-throat nature of the big city, where people will manipulate and murder for their own ends. This is the hunting ground of the elite and the desperate, a very different place to where Pip grew up.

Wemmick's response to Pip is also interesting, as he says that he doesn't think there is much difference between doing something bad to an enemy and doing something bad because there is something to gain from it. Wemmick is naturalised to the surroundings and nature of London, showing that one can become used to the conniving and duplicitous city. Wemmick leaves Pip at Barnard's Inn and Pip meets Herbert Pocket who turns out to be the "pale young gentleman" he met and fought at Satis House.

Chapter 22

Pip immediately forms a lasting companionship with Herbert. Eventually Pip arranges to share lodgings with Herbert at Barnard's Inn and their friendship becomes a rare example of genuine bourgeoisie camaraderie. This is further shown by the amiable nickname "Handel" granted by Herbert to Pip, defining their relationship as exceedingly authentic in contrast to the other transactional and superficial exchanges between other upper-class characters. Furthermore, Herbert's "wonderfully hopeful" and honest nature is commended by Dickens to be somewhat similar to that of Joe. This is contrasted with the increasingly self-important attitudes of Pip who secretly reprimands Herbert's compassion as a weakness in the rapacious London society, assuming that in acquiring these genuine features "he would never be very successful or rich."

Nonetheless, whilst getting along famously, Herbert sympathetically educates Pip on the "ways of politeness" and etiquette of the upper class. This is most prominent in their dining at Barnard's Inn as Herbert politely corrects Pip's manner of eating by informing him that "the spoon is not generally used over-hand, but under" and that "society as a body does not expect one to be so strictly conscientious in emptying one's glass, as to turn it bottom upwards with the rim on one's nose." In expressing these mannerisms that differ greatly to the unregulated dining of Pip's life on the marshes and even more drastically to the "dog-like" eating of the convict earlier in the novel, Dickens exhibits the **bourgeoisie tendencies to prioritise displays of etiquette and leisure over instinctual or essential acts of survival.** However, these arbitrary mannerisms are societally substantiated with seemingly logical explanations to "get at your mouth better" or to avoid "accidents." Dickens exposes the absurd nature of these rules, suggesting that they are utilised by the upper classes as **barriers to entry to upper-class society that need to be overcome by the lower classes if they want to ascend the social hierarchy.**

Additionally, Herbert divulges to Pip the true story of Miss Havisham's life, contextualising the reasons for her unconventional, depressing lifestyle where she is "transfixed" in the moments before her wedding. In articulating the tragic story of her prematurely halted wedding, Miss Havisham's status as an ageing, unmarried woman becomes evident in being a contributing factor to her reclusive lifestyle and subsequent lack of autonomy. More so, her manipulative endeavours in having "brought up [Estella] [...] to wreak revenge on all the male sex" is determined to be a result of the heartbreak inflicted on her 25 years ago by the man that she "passionately loved" who left her at the altar – leaving a mere letter that "heartlessly broke the marriage off." In telling this story, Dickens gives context to Miss Havisham's peculiar existence and intentions for Estella, prefacing a further exploration of beauty and wealth.

Chapters 23, 24, 25, and 26

Pip goes to Matthew Pocket's house to be tutored and meets his fellow students: Drummle and Startop. The two have opposite personalities: Startop is a "lively bright young fellow," while Drummle is an heir to a baronetcy and a "sulky" man. Pip is also introduced to the Pocket family, whose household seems to be run by their servants.

Returning to Mr Jaggers' office, Pip becomes further acquainted with Wemmick and is invited to dine at his house. Dickens accentuates the fact that Wemmick is forced to separate his private life and work life – existing as a "dry," "hard" businessman at work, yet jovially taking pride in his self-made "little wooden cottage in the midst of plots of garden" and enjoying a wholesome private life of gardening and caring for his elderly parent at home.

Unlike proletarian workers such as Joe, who are intrinsically bound to their physical labour, this separation between private life and work life is depicted as a privilege for the wealthy. This is also exemplified by Jaggers who "washe[s] his clients off," cleaning his hands rigorously after working as a lawyer in court to rid himself of the burdens of his occupation when transitioning back to his personal life, symbolising the removal of the stain of his working life.

Finally, Pip is invited to dinner at Mr Jaggers house along with Herbert, Drummle, and Startop. Through the general disputes over money and competitive "boast[s]" made by all men including Pip – bragging of his "tendency to lavish expenditure" and endeavours to "patronise Herbert" – Dickens displays the **contagious nature of self-importance and desire for superiority** which **influences shifts in Pip's sense of morality.** As such, he becomes a **reflection of his socio-cultural environment,** transforming from a guileless and virtuous young boy (during his childhood) to an exceedingly ambitious young man, driven by a hunger to maintain financial and social superiority.

Chapter 27

Biddy sends notice that Joe is coming to London with Mr Wopsle and would be delighted to meet with Pip. Upon receiving this news "not with pleasure" but instead with "some mortification, and a keen sense of incongruity," Pip becomes anxious about Joe's visit, dreading the thought of being ridiculed for his association with Joe by Bentley Drummle.

As such, Dickens emphasises Pip's current **prioritising of the opinions and perspectives of other gentlemen over his once honest relationship with Joe** and former pride in his "common" aspirations of becoming a blacksmith.

Joe's behaviour is awkward and tense as he calls Pip sir, which exemplifies his discomfort in being surrounded by the intimidating upper-class society which deems him inferior. Pip criticises Joe for his "utterly preposterous" clothing and lack of genteel etiquette, having "dropped so much more than he ate, and pretended that he hadn't dropped it." Pip only recently was in the same clothing and had the same mannerisms, thus Dickens engenders a sense of unjust hypocrisy and highlights Pip's shame of his roots. Contrasting Pip's rapid societal advancement, Joe's visit serves as a reminder of Pip's past life and the stagnant nature of life at the forge in comparison to the bustling city atmosphere in London, noting that everything back at his old home was "much the same as when" he had left.

> **Allude:** to say something indirectly.

Pip is told that Mr Wopsle had left the church to become an actor in London. Here, Dickens potentially **alludes** to the façade employed not only in Mr Wopsle's character, but also in Pip's theatrical disguise in occupying the role of an upper-class gentleman. At the end of their meeting Joe informs Pip that Miss Havisham has requested his presence at Satis House as "Estella has come home and would be glad to see him." Suddenly, Pip's disagreeable attitude is relinquished and Pip realises his rudeness and hopes that Joe will stay longer. Thus, Dickens purports that the **upper class entertain those "lower" than them only when it is in the interest of their personal gain.** Miss Havisham entertained Pip in his childhood as a test dummy for Estella, Mr Jaggers looks after Pip because he is paid to do so. The upper class then is characterised as cold, ambitious, and self-centred. Joe, on the other hand, has come to London at his own expense to visit a child he raised out of the goodness of his heart for no benefit.

In parting, Joe acknowledges the prevailing influence of one's environment on their perception saying "you won't find half so much fault in me if you think of me in my forge dress, with my hammer in my hand" before departing London. Joe also uses an extensive metalsmithing metaphor in his parting, indicating that the division and awkwardness between the two of them is not Pip's fault, merely the nature of life: "Pip, dear old chap, life is made of ever so many partings welded together, as I may say, and one man's a blacksmith, and one's a whitesmith, and one's a goldsmith, and one's a coppersmith. Diwisions among such must come, and must be met as they come. If there's been any fault at all today, it's mine." This demonstrates Joe's morally good nature despite Pip's arrogance and cruelty in his treatment of him.

Chapter 28

Pip returns to Satis House to visit Miss Havisham, and more importantly to see Estella. He intends to stay at his old home with Joe, Biddy, and Mrs Joe as an act of "repentance" for his previous hostility towards Joe. Yet he becomes entangled by his own self-centredness and preoccupation with his anticipation to see Estella, so he resolves to stay at the Blue Boar instead. This once again signifies his **prioritisation of ambition, wealth, and desire over genuine human connection.**

He returns home in a carriage accompanied by two convicts which reminds him of the frightening formative encounter he had with the convict on the marshes. As such, Dickens reestablishes Pip's infantile guilt and alludes to the inescapable nature of Pip's proletarian upbringing, still following him throughout his hierarchical ascent.

Pip recognises one of the convicts to be the strange man who had gifted him with "two one pound notes" in chapter 10. Moreover, through the conversation between the two convicts Dickens alludes to their association with the convict Pip helped at the beginning of the narrative, subtly **foreshadowing the revelation of Pip's "liberal benefactor"** towards the end of the novel.

Acknowledging Pip's drastic change in "the course of nature" and "circumstance" at this point in the novel, Dickens emphasises that his name has become one of the last remaining parts of his past identity, demonstrated through Pip's fear that the convict would recognise him only by hearing his name, yet otherwise had "no suspicion of [his] identity."

Arriving at the Blue Boar, Pip learns through the local newspaper that Mr Pumblechook has taken credit for being "the founder of [Pip's] fortunes." Dickens not only articulates the shifts in attitudes of others towards Pip proceeding his rise to fortune, but additionally highlights the shame and dissatisfaction experienced by Pip as a result of the disingenuous relationships that have surfaced now that he is ascending the class hierarchy.

Chapter 29

Pip visits Satis House with an arrogant disposition, believing himself to be a "hero" destined to be married to Estella. Dickens further evokes the notion of Estella's "strong possession" over Pip, rendering her beauty and wealth to provoke Pip's desires. As elucidated throughout these chapters, Dickens articulates that **physical beauty and money become inextricably bound in the perverse values of the bourgeoisie** – essentially, Pip's enchantment by Estella's "irresistible" physical beauty becomes wedded to his yearning to gain capital and social status.

Yet, in bearing witness to Estella's newly acquired womanly beauty, Pip's admiration renders him inferior to her unattainable charm, evoking the same feelings of humiliation and dissatisfaction that he once felt as a "coarse and common boy." This initiates Pip's realisation of how his rapacious "hankerings after money and gentility" are inextricably linked with the desire for Estella. Through this connection between money and beauty, **Dickens begins to introduce the perpetual dissatisfaction bred from an insatiable yearning for these superficial markers of value**, which are eventually deemed **unable to fulfil one's genuine contentment.**

When Pip enters Satis House he has "lighter boots than of yore." This directly contrasts the once common "thick boots" he wore whilst entering Miss Havisham's estate for the first time. This physically emblematises his outward transition into a more honourable gentleman of 19th century society.

Inefficacious: an undesirable result.

Pyrrhic: a victory that is won at too great a cost to be worthwhile.

Reification: to make something that is immaterial, material.

Estella's continual treatment of Pip as a mere "boy" despite his rise in fortune demonstrates the **inefficacious** result of his **pyrrhic** achievements of upper-class gentility. It also further portrays the vicarious effects of Miss Havisham's manipulations of Estella as she cruelly endeavours to break Pip's heart. Repeating the rigorous demand "love her, love her, love her!" Miss Havisham proceeds to enforce this malevolent game of manipulation, subsequently adhered to by Pip in his affirmations "I love her, I love her, I love her!"

Dickens also begins to allude to the **interchangeable nature of the subject and the object in this capitalistic society** in which **Estella is objectified as an embodiment of beauty and wealth.** Decorating Estella with "the most beautiful jewels," Miss Havisham manufactures Estella as a **reification** of aesthetic elegance, so much so that she is denied any autonomy and is instead objectified as a "pawn" in Miss Havisham's game. Thematically, this is explored by Dickens to illuminate the **objectification of the female figure in a society that values material wealth over individual autonomy.**

Pip is informed that Estella will visit London, which excites him as he anticipates his optimistic future with her. Much like how Pip assumes Miss Havisham is his benefactor, he again boyishly and arrogantly assumes that Estella is meant to be wed to him.

Chapter 30

When Pip starts his journey back to London he is ridiculed by Mr Trabb's assistant for his significant change in appearance since his last visit. This provokes within Pip an "aggravation" and humiliation as Dickens further proves Pip's dissatisfaction with his life despite displaying his "distinguished" status.

Upon arriving back at Barnard's Inn in London, Pip divulges the details of his trip to Herbert, expressing his adoration for the "beautiful and most elegant" Estella. Pip learns of Herbert's engagement to a young lady of lower status than himself named Clara. Through Herbert's attainable engagement to Clara, Dickens creates a drastic contrast between Pip's fanciful desires of marrying Estella and Herbert's realistic aspirations which will likely lead to a more fulfilling outcome.

Chapter 31

Pip and Herbert attend Mr Wopsle's amateur play, through which Dickens establishes an **ironic** juxtaposition between Pip's artificial façade in occupying the role of a bourgeoisie gentleman and Mr Wopsle's somewhat **hyperbolic** parody in occupying his role in the performance of Hamlet. As such, **Dickens suggests an artificiality to the role of the upper-class gentleman in Victorian society.**

Ironic: something humorous because the situation is different to reality.

Chapter 32

After receiving a note from Estella ordering him to meet her in London, Pip, in great anticipation, arrives at the coach office four to five hours early.

Hyperbole: a literary device which uses exaggeration to make something seem more extreme.

He encounters Wemmick whilst waiting for Estella, who takes him to Newgate jail to speak with a client. Through Pip's discomfort in the dismal surroundings of the prison, Dickens emphasises Pip's sense of superiority over the prisoners, perceiving himself (due to his distinguished status) tainted by the unsavoury surroundings of "prison and crime."

By ridding himself of the remnant "prison dust" air in order to meet Estella, Dickens orchestrates a striking contrast between Pip's disdainful perception of the prison and his enchanted desire of Estella, believing with "absolute abhorrence" that being at all associated with the grimy prison would render him undesirable in the eyes of the "delicately beautiful" Estella.

Chapter 33

Estella finally meets Pip in London. Estella's lack of autonomy is clearly shown through the succinct sentences of Estella's instructions, such as "I am to have a carriage, and you are to take me. This is my purse, and you are to pay my charges out of it." She even explicitly states that "We have no choice, you and I, but to obey our instructions. We are not to follow our own devices." Through this it becomes evident that Estella's demanding instructions have been enforced vicariously from Miss Havisham and she is self-aware of her own imprisonment in her beauty and status.

They arrive at Richmond where Estella will stay with a powerful lady of status. Dickens demonstrates the power of wealth, as Miss Havisham's affluence has granted Estella the privilege of being effortlessly absorbed into the ranks of bourgeoisie society. Yet this additionally continues to establish the **dichotomy between autonomy and objectification of the female figure.** Whilst Miss Havisham's wealth permits Estella to receive an upper-class education and life of "variety and admiration," it simultaneously **facilitates her objectification,** valued no more than an inanimate jewel to be admired or envied and married off.

This is particularly evident in the statement "I and the Jewels," in which the subject and object become somewhat mutable as **Estella is reified into an embodiment of her mother's wealth and aspirations,** becoming intrinsically bound to the objects of her affluence. As such, the capitalised "Jewels" highlight the connection between economics and beauty.

Pip and Estella get into a subtle dispute in which she says that "you must not expect me to go to school to *you*; I must talk in my own way," focalising on Pip's insubstantial foundational education despite now being a gentleman. Through this Dickens emphasises Pip's alienation, both from the wealthy world and the working-class one. He has become estranged from his former working-class life, his wealth eliminating his relationship to meritocratic labour. Yet due to the contrasting upbringings of Pip and Estella and his lack of an upper-class childhood, he is also alienated from the bourgeoisie world – made clear by the cruel Estella.

Chapter 34

Pip parts with Estella and proceeds to summarise the following period of his life in which his "lavish habits," arrogant ambition, and self-centred greed drive him into debt. Pip is becoming deeply dissatisfied with the perpetual disillusionment of his upper-class lifestyle. In acknowledging his negative influence on Herbert and poor treatment of Joe and Biddy, his conscience grows as he begins to contemplate the genuine satisfaction that he could have achieved from an honest working-class life on the forge. Thus, Pip is beginning to gain further maturity and understanding of the true nature of life.

Pip then receives a letter informing him of Mrs Joe's death, marking a significant moment in Pip's development and maturation as his thoughts are "haunted" by "the figure of [his] sister" infiltrating his mind with a constant reminder of his proletarian past.

Chapter 35

Pip returns home for the funeral, attempting to comfort Joe and Biddy, acknowledging their strained relationship, and promising, despite Biddy's scepticism, to return soon. Yet, as he leaves, amongst the revelatory imagery of "mists [...] rising" and an admission from the narrator that Biddy's scepticism was warranted, Dickens elucidates Pip's alienation from his working-class origins and illustrates his **distancing from the morally righteous ideals of the proletariat embodied by Joe and Biddy.**

Chapter 36

Chapter 36 marks a grand milestone in Pip's life as he and Herbert "come of age," turning twenty one and officially entering adulthood. Looking forward to his birthday "with a crowd of speculations and anticipations," Pip finally gains access to his fortune, receiving a rate of five hundred pounds per year. However, despite this large sum he remains embroiled in emerging debts.

On this "**auspicious**" day, Pip hopes that Jaggers will reveal the identity of his benefactor, who he still believes to be Miss Havisham. Yet, he is disappointed as Jaggers refuses to reveal his employer's identity, merely reiterating his initial statement that "it might be years hence when that person appeared." Despite Pip's disappointment with the outcome of the meeting, he invites Jaggers to join Herbert and himself for dinner which renders the evening "uncomfortable" and dull. Pip notes that while Jaggers is "a thousand times better informed and cleverer than Wemmick" he would have "a thousand times rather have had Wemmick to dinner." Dickens alludes to Pip's **burgeoning realisation of the value of genuine camaraderie and human connection over wealth and status.**

Auspicious: a good sign, promising success and fortune.

Pip's arrogance and delusion are evident as Pip believes Jaggers is jealous that he isn't in on the secret of Pip's marriage to Estella. Pip believes this must be the reason that Jaggers did not tell Pip of his benefactor's identity. This delineates the extent to which Pip **deceives himself, egotistically associating his own economic and hierarchical advancement with destined romance.** Pip's **major character flaw of ambition** continues to drive his egotistical and deluded behaviour to his own detriment throughout the novel.

Chapter 37

Receiving his prosperous income, Pip admirably decides to help Herbert, who according to Pip has "no money, and finds it difficult and disheartening to make a beginning." Whilst at Jaggers' office Pip seeks advice from Wemmick who initially offers a cynical financial opinion to "never invest portable property in a friend," essentially dissuading Pip from helping Herbert. However, Wemmick gives Pip a different and entirely opposite opinion when they meet at his castle and says he intends to help Pip.

As such, Dickens further establishes the ability of upper-class individuals to separate their work and private lives to avoid ethical implications in either domain of life. This is exemplified in Wemmick's statement, "Walworth is one place, and the office is another. [...] They must not be confounded together." It also establishes the idea of the façade worn by high society and the **duplicitous nature of the upper class.**

In a **convivial** spirit, Wemmick supports Pip in his endeavour to buy Herbert a partnership in the business of a merchant. However, Pip keeps his involvement secret from Herbert. Through this kind-hearted yet covert plan, Dickens alludes to the potential good that can be done through capitalistic endeavours, yet also shows how this is tainted by the lies Pip must tell in the process. Nonetheless, in articulating that Pip's "expectations had done some good to somebody," Dickens illuminates the potential for positive results to be born from wealth and status. He also demonstrates that **Pip has genuinely matured, exhibiting a greater sense of compassion and empathy.**

Convivial: friendly or lively.

Chapter 38

The narrator dedicates the entirety of chapter 38 to his beloved Estella who he falsely yet whole-heartedly believes to be a "prize reserved for" himself in marriage. Beginning to realise his perplexing relationship with Estella is manipulative, Pip grows disheartened and angry over his diminishing hopes of being destined to marry the object of his desires.

Pip spends a considerable amount of time attending to Estella and obliging her requests to accompany her everywhere; however, he discerns that Estella is often exploiting him "to tease other admirers." Through suggestions that the rigid relationship between Estella and Pip was "forced upon" them by Miss Havisham, Dickens depicts the lack of autonomy afforded to Estella in her relationships as a product of Miss Havisham's authoritative control and affluence.

Pip's frustration grows as he witnesses Estella's cruel and insulting treatment of other suitors as she remains predominantly indifferent towards him, leaving him "entirely out of the question." When Pip accompanies Estella back to Satis House, they return to the sombre, decaying estate where Pip begins to see Miss Havisham's obsession with Estella's beauty and her intentions for Estella "to wreak [her] revenge on men."

In a revelatory spiral, Pip suddenly becomes aware of Miss Havisham's "malicious" endeavours for Estella "to attract and torment" him. He is only consoled by the deluded assumption that he will one day marry Estella, claiming the "prize" that he believes to be destined for him. Through this, Dickens elucidates Miss Havisham's overt manipulation, yet simultaneously emphasises the self-centredness and arrogance of Pip in his blind assumptions that he will marry Estella. In objectifying Estella as a "prize" to be won, Dickens conveys how the **blatant disregard for individual identity is manifested in the perverse moral values of the bourgeoisie** of which Pip has obtained through his rise to be a gentleman.

At Satis House, the two women fight and Estella blames her adoptive mother for her own "cold heart [...] never yielding either to anger or tenderness" not only towards her male suitors but also towards Miss Havisham herself. Miss Havisham reprimands Estella for being ungrateful, neglecting to acknowledge that it was her bitter upbringing of Estella as a "puppet" to exercise revenge on the male sex that has rendered Estella to be the same. Through Estella's rebuttal that "the success is not mine, the failure is not mine, but the two together make me," Dickens accentuates the **absence of an individual identity in the figure of Estella,** who is forced to be an **embodiment of the perpetually dissatisfied and objectified upper-class woman.** Pip's expectations and hopes of an engagement announcement begin to deteriorate and his discontentment seethes after learning that Estella is being courted by the "deficient, ill-tempered, lowering, stupid fellow" Bentley Drummle.

Resenting the circumstances of his dwindling chances of marrying Estella, Pip confronts Estella regarding her relationship with "a man so generally despised as Drummle." She dismisses his objections, instead expressing her intentions only to "deceive and entrap him" as well as many others, with the singular exception of Pip himself (yet another manipulation). Instead of feeling reassured, Pip is further disheartened as he starts to see through Estella's manipulations. Dickens artfully depicts Pip's fateful burden through the metaphor that a heavy "ceiling [was] dropped upon [him]" under which he was crushed.

Chapter 39

This chapter delineates a drastic change in the entire trajectory of Pip's life and thus the narrative of *Great Expectations*. Pip undergoes pivotal revelations that challenge his perceptions and beliefs. In fact, all of his established social values as a gentleman are uprooted by the unveiling of his benefactor's identity.

Years have gone by and Pip is now 23 and has moved out of Barnard's Inn to live in the Temple with Herbert. Alone on a "wretched [...] stormy and wet" evening, Pip becomes frightened by the sound of "a footstep on the stair." Pip connects the noise he hears with "the footstep of [his] dead sister." This foreshadows the person's identity, as Dickens alludes to Pip's past life returning to haunt him.

The ominous atmosphere creates a foreboding sense of chaos as the rain "dashed against the windows" and "smoke came rolling down the chimney," continuing the omnipresent motif of the physical environment influencing the events of the narrative. This same **pathetic fallacy** is used in the beginning of the novel when Pip first meets the convict, thus the return of the stormy weather foreshadows the reemergence of this character in the novel. As the storm causes all of the lights to be "blown out," the prevailing darkness of the room and the stairwell evokes a visceral sense of uncertainty, reminiscent of the uncertainty of the ambiguous origins of Pip's fortune.

Pathetic fallacy: when human emotions are expressed through inanimate things.

Pip sees a man positioned at the bottom of the stairs, "beneath" Pip who remains at the top. Through this, Dickens **symbolically suggests that the mysterious intruder is of a lower hierarchical status than Pip** by condemning him to a physically lower level, enveloped by darkness.

This **persisting symbol of "darkness"** is repeatedly employed by Dickens throughout this chapter, emulating the **uncertain and ominous nature** in which the man approaches. Pip's lamp only illuminates the stairwell with a small circle of light so he can only see fragments of the convict. Pip is frightened by what he sees, describing the man as having "a rough outer coat," "long iron grey hair [that] grew only" on the sides of his "furrowed and bald" head, and "large brown veinous hands." The minimal and constricted presence of light **metaphorically displays Pip's closed-mindedness and narrow world view,** which is further shown through Pip's prejudiced descriptions of the man.

Pip finally recognises the stranger to be the convict who he had encountered on the marshes on the fateful day recounted in chapter 1 and immediately assumes that he had found Pip to thank him. The ex-convict (later known to be called Magwitch) reveals his identity as Pip's liberal benefactor, expressing "Pip, dear boy, I've made a gentleman on you!" He recounts how he made his fortune as a "sheep-farmer [...] in a solitary hut" devoting all of his money and effort to making Pip a gentleman in return for his **altruism** on that fateful day on the marshes. To this, Pip is confounded with the injustice with which he has treated the man. Pip discovers that the convict is now a fugitive, facing potential execution, and despite being conflicted by the "perception of [his] wretchedness," Pip tries to help his benefactor. He provides Magwitch with food and shelter which **draws a distinct parallel between this moment and their first encounter on the marshes.**

Pip becomes overwhelmed with the reality of his disillusionment in believing he was destined to marry Estella. With the "sharpest and deepest" remorse he realises the futility of his suffering at Satis House and hollow endeavours for hierarchical ascension at the cost of his relationships with Joe and Biddy. Anticipating the uncertain turmoil of his future, Pip retires to sleep and awakens in the morning to the "thick black darkness" concocted by the wrathful storm through which Dickens **foreshadows the impending turbulence and challenges that await Pip.**

> **Altruism:** selfless concern or acts of kindness with no expectation of reward.

Part 3

Chapter 40

The reappearance of Pip's convict – now known to be his benefactor Abel Magwitch – forces Pip to confront the reality of his fortune being provided to him by a fugitive. Pip decides to help the convict who is at risk of being hanged if captured. By providing the convict with help, Dickens establishes a prevailing conflict between Pip's fear of and fear for his benefactor. While Pip is still frightened of Magwitch, he feels obliged to ensure that Magwitch is not caught which would weigh on Pip's moral conscience. Pip sees the potential hanging of Magwitch to be his responsibility and regards himself as Magwitch's potential murderer. Therefore, Pip uses the alias Uncle Provis to conceal Magwitch's identity from others.

Parallels are once again drawn between Pip's first encounter with Magwitch and his now drastically different life, which becomes somewhat pervaded by the figures of his past. Evident in Magwitch's eating "like a hungry old dog" and playing "a complicated kind of Patience with a ragged pack of cards of his own," Dickens establishes these parallels in complicating Pip's perceptions of the upper-class and lower-class values, disturbed by the revelation of his own fortune being provided by a lowly convict.

Chapter 41

Obliging to help Magwitch and with the assistance of his companions Herbert and Wemmick, Pip resolves to temporarily hide him at the "quiet lodging" of Herbert's fiancée Clara. Through this collaborative effort, Dickens illuminates the **themes of friendship and loyalty,** which he commends to be genuine and fulfilling pursuits.

Throughout the chapters, the improper cadences of Magwitch's dialogue in phrases such as "look'ee here" and the repeated use of "fur" instead of "far" maintain his animalistically low status, which Pip becomes confused by and ashamed of. Pip also realises that he is "heavily in debt" to this man, who is of considerably lower hierarchical status. Pip pities Magwitch, concluding that he must stop taking money from him and take his finances into his own hands. This provokes Pip's contemplation that he "would have far far rather have worked at the forge" than face the jarring consequences of his actions throughout the novel, foregrounding the recurring internal conflict in the novel.

Chapter 42

Abel Magwitch recounts his troubled upbringing as an orphan and his criminal past driven by a desperate necessity for survival, a concept which starkly contrasts the leisurely lives of the bourgeoisie. He tells Pip of a prominent and merciless person pivotal to his life of crime, named Compeyson.

Compeyson is characterised as an educated gentleman invested in a career of "swindling, handwriting forging, [and] stolen bank-note passing" who manipulated Magwitch during their shared crimes, resulting in the arrest of both men.

In relaying the details of Magwitch and Compeyson's court hearing, Dickens **accentuates the injustices and biases of the legal system,** in which those with an upper-class education and appearance are favoured over those of working-class backgrounds. The author condemns how this serves to perpetuate and validate the social class divide, operating under the prejudice of the Victorian **societal superstructure**.

> **The societal superstructure:** a societal convention in Marxist ideology, suggesting that the dominant institutional bodies (e.g education, politics, law, and religion) reflect the interests of the ruling/upper class and thus perpetuate and legitimise the social class divide.

This is evinced through Magwitch's frustrations that Compeyson, a well-dressed, "well brought up" gentleman was treated with a respectable sense of justice, receiving a sentence of only seven years despite having instigated the crime. This is compared to Magwitch himself, "the elder, ill brought up" accomplice without the privileges of an educated gentleman, who received a fourteen-year sentence. This validates the notion of lower-class individuals being of inferior value to upper-class society and perpetuates the endless cycle of poverty.

It is also noted by Magwitch that Compeyson had manipulated another man named Arthur who had gained a large sum of money from a "bad thing with a rich lady some years afore," which the reader can infer is about Miss Havisham. Furthermore, Magwitch yearns to seek revenge against his ex-accomplice.

A series of revelations take place where Compeyson is revealed to have been the fellow escaped convict that Pip had initially encountered in the churchyard many years ago. He is also surprisingly revealed to be Miss Havisham's lover who left her on her wedding day. Arthur is revealed to be Miss Havisham's half-brother who was an accomplice to the scheme.

As such, the previously separate worlds which Pip inhabits begin to unveil their connections, blurring the once rigid boundaries of the Victorian social hierarchy that distinguished the upper and lower classes. More so, Dickens discredits these societal constructs, instead condoning friendship and loyalty as a more reliable source of fulfilling human connection.

Chapter 43

After hearing Magwitch's story Pip is determined to get him out of the country. But first he intends to see Estella and Miss Havisham one last time. He travels to his home village and runs into Bentley Drummle in the Blue Boar. They have a very stiff, uncomfortable conversation where neither is clear of the other's intention. But the insinuation is that Drummle is there to marry or court Estella which infuriates Pip.

Interestingly there is a lot of descriptive focus on their shoes, "here Mr Drummle looked at his boots and I looked at mine, and then Mr Drummle looked at my boots, and I looked at his." Shoes have repetitively surfaced throughout the novel as a symbol of class.

Pip's once thick boots were a sign of his lowly status, whereas his new thin boots are a sign of his entry into upper-class society. Here, Drummle and Pip are weighing each other up, using their shoes as a symbol of status.

Throughout their conversation, Drummle seems to imply he knows of Pip's lowly upbringing and thinks himself better than Pip. Again, Dickens drives home the message that despite his riches, new clothes, and manners, Pip is always deemed one step below those who are born to titles and money, and that despite Pip's great expectations and ambition he can never fully realise his goal.

Chapter 44

Pip goes to Satis House to bid farewell to Estella and beg Miss Havisham to continue to fund the farce that helped Herbert to obtain his merchant business which she agrees to do. In this meeting, the truth of Miss Havisham and her manipulations of Pip are fully revealed. Pip admits that Miss Havisham's manipulations worked, saying "I am as unhappy as you can ever have meant me to be" and asks her if she thought it was a kind thing to do.

Pip then professes his love for Estella. She is completely indifferent, telling him that she never pretended to show feelings for him, and that it was all his delusion. He begs her not to marry Drummle, but she insists that it is already organised. Pip continues to tell Estella how horrible Drummle is and that she could marry so many better men than him, but she is unmoved by his pleas. This shows her lack of agency and her resignation to living her current life in which she is merely a puppet for those around her. However, this act of marrying Drummle appears to be Estella's one act of independence. She says that Miss Havisham "would have [her] wait, and not marry yet" but she has made the choice anyway, stating she is sick of her life. Estella's life is filled with cruelty and is at the behest of others. Marrying Drummle, the hair to a baronetcy, may afford her freedoms that she has never had before.

In a final goodbye, Pip confesses the extent of his affections for Estella, shocking them all. Estella's education of men is that they are all deceitful, wicked creatures to be used and manipulated lest they hurt her. Her whole life had been about learning to attract gentlemen so she can cause them pain when she leaves them coldheartedly. Since that is her experience, Pip's heartfelt pledge of his love changes her slightly, looking at Pip with "incredulous wonder." After this, Pip is so distraught that he walks all the way back to London where he receives a distressing note from Wemmick that says "don't go home."

Chapter 45

Pip heads straight to a seedy inn where he spends a rather distressing night before heading to Wemmick's castle. Here he receives jarring news that Compeyson is alive and has come to London. Wemmick tells him this information in secret at great risk to himself, showing the true companionship between Pip and Wemmick. He further tells Pip that Magwitch is at Herbert's fiancée's house which is close to a river. From there he suggests that he can place Magwitch on a boat leaving England.

Chapter 46

Pip arrives at Clara's house to find Magwitch. He meets Clara for the first time and sees the merit in the loving and warm companionship she has with Herbert, saying that he "would not have undone the engagement between her and Herbert for all the money in the pocket-book [he] had never opened." This depicts the maturity Pip has gained in seeing the true value of loving human companionship over money and status. Although neither Clara nor Herbert are wealthy, they have a fulfilling life together.

Pip tells Magwitch and Herbert everything Wemmick has told him except for the fact Compeyson is still alive, deciding to withhold that information from him lest he seek revenge. They decide that the boys will drive the boat themselves to sneak Magwitch out of the city, so Pip goes to buy a boat so he can practise driving it. However, he can't help but feel like he is still being watched. Throughout this chapter Pip's attitude is changing towards Magwitch, and he even notes that Magwitch has seemed to "soften."

Chapter 47

Pip is in trouble with his debts as he feels he shouldn't spend Magwitch's money. To deter his thoughts of Estella and Drummle getting married he meets Mr Wopsle at the theatre. Wopsle tells Pip that he thought he saw one of the convicts from the marshes in the audience. This terrifies Pip and confirms his suspicions of being watched.

Chapter 48

When dining at Mr Jaggers' house, Pip notices similarities between Molly, Jagger's maid (described as a "wild beast tamed" and perceived to have had a violent criminal past) and Estella. Pip notes that "her hands were Estella's hands, and her eyes were Estella's eyes."

Additionally, through the aligning stories of both Molly and Magwitch's pasts, Pip concludes that Molly is Estella's biological mother and that Magwitch is in fact Estella's father. Through this development, **Dickens questions the validity of the social structures that Pip has come to understand.** This is contrary to his previous assumptions that Estella was a high-born woman of upper-class parentage, thus Pip is now shocked to learn that her origins are of even lesser social status than his own, sparking a **reflection on his misconceptions of social value.** Yet Pip's love for Estella remains unchanged, despite her humble origins and her imminent marriage to Bentley Drummle, further subverting the rigidity of hierarchical ideals. Similarly, his affections towards Magwitch continue to develop.

Chapter 49

Pip returns to Satis House which is now "sadder" and "more remote" than ever in the absence of Estella. Miss Havisham desperately grovels for forgiveness and admits her guilt for manipulating both Pip and Estella. She desperately confesses that she is "not all stone," repeatedly questioning "what have I done!" Dickens, for the first time in the novel, attributes a human sense of remorse to the previously "heartless" and "cold" Miss Havisham.

This further destabilises Pip's understanding of his relationships throughout the narrative and **contributes to his growing comprehension that true satisfaction can only be achieved by genuine human relationships.** In addition, **Dickens also emphasises the perpetual dissatisfaction of the bourgeoisie lifestyle,** articulating how after her games of manipulation have failed to fulfil her pursuit for revenge against the male sex, Miss Havisham now **desperately seeks satisfaction in the pursuit of forgiveness, realising the value of honest human connection** at a point when it is evidently too late to remedy her mistakes.

"Kneeling at [Pip's] feet" Miss Havisham's manic expressions of "unworthiness" instigate a **drastic shift in the power dynamic** between the two characters. In granting forgiveness to Miss Havisham, despite her cruel treatment of Pip, **he demonstrates a matured capacity for empathy** contrary to his own bitterness at the peak of his process in becoming a gentleman.

While Pip is walking in the yard, Miss Havisham becomes enveloped in a "great flaming [...] whirl of fire," her dress having caught a stray ember from the fireplace. She runs towards Pip "shrieking." **This fire becomes symbolic of her burning guilt and raging self-destruction** that ultimately leads to her demise, attesting to Dickens' suggestions of **inevitable ruin and dissatisfaction in upholding the spiteful ideals of the upper class.**

Having been gravely injured, yet still remaining alive, Miss Havisham meets the fateful consequences of her manipulation as she is "laid upon the great table" amongst the festering decay of her past. She lifelessly repeats her desperate confessions of guilt "in a low solemn voice."

Comparatively, this fate mirrors that of Mrs Joe Gargery, **alluding to the unbiased nature of illness and demise,** unprejudiced towards wealth and status. Subsequently, Pip's own injuries, being "a good deal burned" on his hands and arms by the fire, **symbolically serve as a physical manifestation of the pain inflicted on** Pip as a result of Miss Havisham's cruelty. Pip's emerging knowledge of the links between the interconnected lives of Miss Havisham and Magwitch disturb his understanding of the previously fixed boundaries of the social hierarchy, and this chapter marks both a physical and mental turning point in how his journey affects him.

Chapters 50, 51, and 52

Injured, Pip returns to London where he learns from Herbert that Magwitch was Molly's former husband. All but confirming him as Estella's father. Pip also gets confirmation from Jaggers, reluctantly, that Molly is in fact her mother.

The tension of the narrative develops as Pip waits for Wemmick's signal to initiate Magwitch's escape and Pip navigates his own emotional connections and moral obligations. Finally, he receives a letter that they are to move Magwitch in two days; however, he also receives a threatening, mysterious letter inviting him to meet on "the old marshes."

Pip heads back to his old home and is overwhelmed with remorse at how he treated his good friend Joe. He remembers how good-natured Joe and Biddy were, thinking, "long-suffering and loving Joe, *you* never complain. Nor you, sweet-tempered Biddy!" On hearing Mr Pumblechook's boasting about being the one to bring Pip to his great fortune, he is struck with how much he took Joe for granted. He sees starkly for the first time the **deceitful nature of vanity associated with class against the humble ever-present goodness of Joe, content in his lower-class role.**

Chapter 53

The character of Orlick is reintroduced by Dickens as a "ghost[like]" figure of Pip's past, embodying a "villain[ous]" attitude of pure evil. Upon meeting Pip at the marshes, Orlick threatens Pip, aggressively expressing "I'm going to have your life" and scolding him for irrational reasons.

Through the "hopelessness" that Pip perceives upon the imminent threat of his death, Dickens evinces a selflessness and an empathetic sense of guilt with which Pip expresses his regrets. He thinks that if he was to die "Estella's father would believe [he] had deserted him," Herbert would resent him, and even "Joe and Biddy would never know how sorry" he had been for his abhorrent treatment towards them.

Through the contrast between Orlick's irrational violence and Pip's newfound appreciation for the authentic, sincere relationships in his life, **Dickens once again commends the value of friendship and loyalty over pointless pursuits of vengeance.** This is further highlighted in Mr Trabb's Boy, Herbert, and Startop rescuing Pip from his almost fatal encounter with Orlick, embodying integrity and loyalty while Orlick embodies a complete negligence of these attributes. It is divulged that the ex-convict Compeyson used Orlick's villainous demeanour in an attempt to ruin both Pip and Magwitch.

Chapter 54

They leave Orlick, not pursuing petty revenge and instead rushing back to London to proceed with the plan to escape via boat with Magwitch. They put the plan into action with the additional help of Startop. The increasingly "dark and mysterious" atmosphere foreshadows the tragic conclusion of their journey.

Part-way through their journey Magwitch is captured by the collaborative forces of police officers and Compeyson (the law and the outlaw), an ironic circumstance. Compeyson drowns after grappling with Magwitch in the water, emphasising Dickens' condemnation of malicious characters.

Compeyson's fate is met in accordance with Magwitch's desires for revenge but not on account of Magwitch's own misconduct. As seen throughout the entirety of the novel, **Dickens establishes this notion that unjust intentions and actions can lead to either a painful fate or character redemption.**

Chapter 55

Following Magwitch's capture and consequent injuries, the evolution in Pip's attitude toward the ex-convict is explicitly accentuated in his expression "my repugnance towards [Magwitch] had all melted away, and in the hunted wounded shackled creature who held my hand in his, I only saw a man who had meant to be my benefactor, and who had felt affectionately, gratefully and generously towards me with great constancy through a series of years." As such, Pip's now entirely sympathetic and affectionate attitude towards Magwitch is elucidated by Dickens to **advance the redemption of Pip's value for loyalty and friendship.** This is even further emphasised in his confessions of deep regret towards his ignorant resentment towards Joe.

Chapter 56

Anticipating the death of Magwitch before his official sentence of death, Pip's wishes to conceal the devastating reality of his own perishing wealth from his benefactor who, even now, takes pride in his contributions to making Pip a gentleman. Ultimately, Magwitch's harmonious acceptance of death portrays his redemption and he is afforded a genuine, authentic relationship with Pip in his final hours. Despite Pip being undeniably alone in contrast to the optimistic romantic endeavours of both Herbert and Wemmick, Pip's loyalty towards Magwitch, visiting him in prison every day and concerning himself deeply with Magwitch's contentment, demonstrates the metamorphosis of Pip's character. **Dickens purports that social status and material wealth are drastically less important than human connection, loyalty, and love.**

Chapter 57

The following final chapters of Charles Dickens' *Great Expectations* act as the **denouement** of the novel, where Pip's turbulent journey of hierarchical ascent and descent culminate. As such, Pip confronts the wrongdoings of his past, reconciling his relationships with loved ones, and subsequently reflects on his life from this newfound perspective. Pip's prevailing loneliness and destitution is manifested in his physical and emotional illness rendering him weak and vulnerable for a significant period of time. In addition to this, the consequences of his past actions and indulgences plague Pip as he is arrested for being severely in debt.

Denouement: the final moments of a piece of literature (play, film, novel, etc.) that brings together all the plot threads.

Indefatigable: to persist at something.

Nonetheless, Joe returns to London to nurse Pip back to health, embodying the epitome of genuine loyalty and unwavering companionship. He again refers to Pip as "old chap" and repeats his "kind-hearted" phrase: "ever the best of friends; ain't us, Pip?" Dickens commends Joe's **indefatigable** tenderness and support towards Pip and rewards Joe's character with a fulfilling fate. Having learnt how to read and write from Biddy, who is revealed to be Joe's new wife, Joe has fulfilled his "great nature" and passion for his craft as a blacksmith which Dickens intimates is **emblematic of a truly fulfilling and satisfying life, without the rapacious, meretricious desires for social superiority.** In juxtaposition to the optimistic destiny of Joe, the villainous Orlick, who ends up in gaol after robbing Mr Pumblechook, emblematises the **opposing fate of a malicious, immoral character** condemned by Dickens through the consequences for his actions.

After recovering from his illness, Pip is informed of Miss Havisham's death and learns with "great joy" that her great fortune had been distributed amongst the Pocket family due to his own expressions to Miss Havisham. Pip additionally learns that Satis House is left to Estella. Immersing themselves in the nostalgia of their once infallible relationship, Pip and Joe "[drive] away together into the country" talking "in the old confidence, and with the old simplicity" as they used to. Yet, when Pip attempts to share with Joe the "circumstances" of Magwitch's demise, Joe refuses, alluding to his unwillingness to revisit the painful memories which would subsequently arise. Through expressing this, Dickens articulates that despite having redeemed his moral values and repaired his fractured relationship with Joe, Pip's resentment and ignorance towards Joe undeniably caused Joe some pain and discomfort. Nonetheless, Joe's compassion allows him to immediately forgive Pip, and in a truly selfless act of love and generosity returns home from London having paid off all of Pip's debts.

Chapter 58

Following Pip's discovery of his debts being paid in full by Joe, Pip returns to his childhood home on the marshes and in the process is treated with a jarring sense of inferiority by various characters (with the exception of Joe and Biddy) now that his "great expectations had all dissolved." In his encounter with Mr Pumblechook, the entitled man looks down on Pip both literally and figuratively in his excessively theatrical manner, giving Pip advice and attempting to assert his superiority in a display of the "toady" attitudes of the middle class.

Pip visits Satis House for what he believes to be the final time and finds it in a disorderly manner and learns that it is up for auction. After doing so, he returns to Biddy and Joe with the intention of mending his relationships and asking for Biddy's hand in marriage.

In a further demonstration of pathetic fallacy, Dickens describes the blue sky and "beautiful [...] peaceful" environment which foreshadow the optimism of Pip's reunion with Joe and Biddy. When they meet, Biddy excitedly announces that she is married to Joe, provoking a genuinely overjoyed reaction from Pip. This displays his truly reformed values and sense of empathy.

Deciding that he must go abroad to work an honest, meritocratic job to repay Joe for his kindness in absolving him of his debt, Pip joins Herbert, taking up his job offer and continuing as "many a year went round" to live an honest, "frugal" life with Herbert and his wife, eventually being able to pay off his debts.

Chapter 59

After eleven years the final chapter takes place, and Pip finally returns to his childhood home. Joe and Biddy are "as strong as ever," incredibly content in their humble lives with two children of their own. In depicting this fulfilling lifestyle of Joe and Biddy, Dickens further commends the satisfaction that results from fostering the honourable value of human connection.

Nonetheless, Pip returns one last time to the **detritus** of Satis House and coincidentally encounters the "solitary figure" of Estella, who is revealed by Dickens to be "leading a most unhappy life [...] separated from her husband, who had used her with great cruelty." This devastating fate is somewhat implied by Dickens to be a consequential result not only of Drummle's "brutality" but also of Estella's objectification and absence of affection or autonomy during her upbringing.

Detritus: waste matter.

In this chance encounter in the overgrown garden of Satis House, Pip describes "the freshness" of Estella's beauty to be diminished, yet still maintaining "its indescribable majesty and its indescribable charm." Estella confesses to Pip that she has often thought of him and expresses that she has always given Pip a place in her heart. Through this, Dickens humanises Estella's character, questioning her previously established heartlessness and resolves Pip and Estella's relationship to conclude as a mutual friendship.

The novel concludes on the hopeful imagery of the "mists [...] rising" yet leaves it on an ambiguous note. As readers, we may interpret this to be suggestive of Pip's newfound clarity, or alternatively of the potential for an optimistic future between Pip and Estella.

Section 4

Character Analysis

Pip

Phillip Pirrip, known throughout the novel as Pip, is the protagonist and narrator of Charles Dickens' *Great Expectations*. He experiences significant development and growth as the narrative progresses, following his maturation from an innocent, young, orphaned boy to the mature and knowledgeable man who narrates his own coming-of-age journey. Considered to be a **bildungsroman**, Dickens' novel focuses on Pip's journey towards fulfilment and self-discovery, grappling with the prevalent themes of social class, morality, ambition, and desire in the hierarchical social climate of early 19th century England.

Bildungsroman: a novel following the narrative of one main character's formative years, moral evolutions, and psychological development.

Dickens masterfully distinguishes between the older version of Pip, who narrates the story, and the character of Pip throughout the novel. This allows him to ascribe a more matured perspective to the narrative voice, who has the hindsight of his past experiences, to influence the recounting of his own story, whilst still allowing the younger character of Pip to provide a firsthand perspective to the events that ensue.

Pip's most prominent character attributes are his ambition and innate moral conscience, with ambition quickly becoming a predominant flaw as the narrative progresses. He continuously aspires for self-improvement after being exposed to the upper-class world which he is initially alienated from in his proletarian upbringing. Subsequently he yearns for social advancement, desiring to escape the shame that he perceives to be associated with the working-class life in the hope of achieving the unattainable prize of Estella's affection.

After inheriting his handsome fortune and titular "great expectations," Pip's previously virtuous moral compass is infected by the capitalistic values of the upper class, prioritising wealth and status over genuine human relationships. This results in Pip's burgeoning arrogance and self-centredness which negatively impacts all of his previously fulfilling relationships, primarily his affectionate companionship with Joe.

Regardless of his evident flaws, Pip both commences and concludes the novel with a sound sense of morality and empathy, fundamentally being **portrayed as a generous character with positive intentions.** He demonstrates this capacity for sympathy and kindness throughout the story, helping others such as Magwitch and Herbert through their own turmoil and challenges.

Ultimately, **Pip's character development delineates the importance of learning to prioritise kindness, loyalty, and innate morality over superficial desires of idealism.**

Multiple revelatory moments occur in Pip's narrative that uproot his simplistic view of the Victorian social hierarchy, causing him to **question his corrupted values** and finally **discover that true worth can only be measured by moral integrity and not wealth or status.**

For example, Pip's discovers that his benefactor is not the rich, upper-class Miss Havisham but in fact the ex-convict Magwitch. He also unveils Estella's extremely low-class biological parentage, Magwitch being her father and the housekeeper Molly being her mother. These discoveries cause Pip to **re-evaluate his personal values and perceptions that had been skewed by the materialistic ideals of upper-class society.** Through these fundamental lessons, Pip concludes his journey as a matured character after having ascended and descended the ultimately arbitrary hierarchy of 19th century society.

Miss Havisham

Miss Havisham is a "ghastly," bitter old woman who lives a life of seclusion, withering away in the decaying confines of her once lavish estate, Satis House. She is one of the most significant characters in the novel as **she emblematises corrupt moral values** and her manipulative influence greatly affects the life of Pip throughout the narrative.

Miss Havisham's very existence is defined by a singular tragic moment from her past; she was betrayed on her wedding day, callously left at the altar after receiving a dismissive letter which left her frozen in time. Since that moment, Miss Havisham has held onto her heartbreak and resentment, stopping her from moving forward. Instead, she remains in her once beautiful, white wedding dress as it fades into a festering yellow fabric, while her body simultaneously withers away into a "corpse-like" shadow of her former self. She also stops all of the clocks in Satis House at twenty minutes to nine, the exact time that she first learned of the betrayal. This shows her stagnation, as she becomes **transfixed in the moment of despair that defines her character.**

Spiralling into a deranged old woman obsessed with exacting "revenge on all of the male sex," Miss Havisham adopts Estella and raises her with cold-heartedness to act as a weapon to pursue her cruel and spiteful endeavours for vengeance against men. Pip soon becomes a victim of these manipulative games as he grows attached to Estella and is ultimately exploited by Miss Havisham for his desires. She repeatedly prompts Pip to fall in love with Estella, simultaneously driving her to break his heart and "have no mercy!"

Thus, in her malevolent manipulation, Miss Havisham serves as a **representation of the immoral ethics and cruelty associated with the values of the bourgeoisie.** Her affluence affords her the ability to ignore the realities of time and everyday concerns that bind the proletariat to the working day, and instead she spends her life indulging in the suffering and struggles of others.

Yet in being granted this perverse sense of autonomy, Miss Havisham's identity as an ageing, unmarried woman in Victorian society renders her representative of the fraught and frightening female figure, seemingly helpless without beauty or a husband to provide her with value in society.

Furthermore, after inflicting so much pain and damage to the lives of those around her, at the end of the novel Miss Havisham finally realises the harm that she has caused in raising Estella to be cold and heartless and exploiting the desires of the once innocent young Pip. This allows Dickens to reinforce the novel's main message – that **moral redemption and integrity** (even of one of the most prolifically antagonistic characters in the novel) **can be achieved through repentance and empathy.** However, by still meeting her tragic fate after her encounter with the fire, Dickens potentially suggests that **the damage caused by her cruelty could not be reversed or absolved by her admissions of guilt alone** but rather would have required her acting upon this pursuit of forgiveness in an attempt to remedy her relationship with Estella. Ultimately, by the time Miss Havisham realises her mistakes, it is too late to repair them despite her still achieving a moral redemption.

Estella

Being adopted by Miss Havisham at a young age, Estella is moulded into a heartless weapon used to exact revenge on the male sex in Miss Havisham's bitter pursuits for indiscriminate vengeance. In abiding by the demands of her adoptive mother, Estella wins Pip's true love and affection whilst deliberately practising Miss Havisham's cruel and insulting ways.

Estella becomes the object of Pip's desires at the hands of Miss Havisham's manipulation, provoking his rapacious "hankerings for money and gentility," which become synonymous with his romantic aspirations. Through this, Estella becomes the **objectified embodiment of beauty and wealth** devoid of any individual identity or autonomy, demonstrating the corrupted values of the bourgeoisie. As such, **Dickens condemns the mutability of the subject and the object that is fostered within upper-class societal ideals,** reifying Estella's physical beauty with Miss Havisham's physical objects of material value, such as her lavish jewels, which become somewhat interchangeable with the identity of Estella.

Through revealing Estella's low-born origins, **Dickens destabilises the impossibility of class ascension** and **questions the rigid capitalistic concept of individual worth and happiness being attached to one's socio-economic status.** Despite being portrayed as an insulting and cruel character, Estella is still somewhat sympathetic throughout the narrative as Dickens attributes her cold-heartedness to be a product of Miss Havisham's manipulation rather than a moral fault of her own. This is exemplified at the very end of the novel when she is reunited with Pip and for the first time is able to express her own emotions saying to Pip, "I have been bent and broken, but – I hope – into a better shape" and confessing that she had always given Pip "a place in [her] heart."

Abel Magwitch

Despite being an essential character to the plot and themes of *Great Expectations*, Magwitch (a.k.a. the convict and Uncle Provis) only really appears at the start and end of the novel. Abel Magwitch is revealed to be the benefactor who provides Pip's fortune despite being a fugitive criminal for much of the story. Through Magwitch, Dickens **destabilises the institutional concept of good and evil,** as despite being a convicted criminal, Magwitch displays the most generosity and genuine gratitude out of all of the characters in the novel. Additionally, his crimes are somewhat validated by Dickens as being a necessary means for survival, rather than malicious endeavours.

Following the initial kindness of Pip in helping Magwitch during their formative encounters on the marshes, Magwitch proceeds to dedicate his life's work to thanking Pip, taking great pride in rewarding his kindness with a handsome fortune, enough to make him a gentleman. However, Pip's subsequent ascent in socio-economic status greatly contrasts the selflessness of Magwitch by obscuring his moral compass and rendering him arrogant and self-centred, indulging in "lavish expenditure" and patronising those around him.

When Magwitch's identity is initially revealed, Pip remains truly shocked and embarrassed that his fortune had come from such lowly, corrupted origins. However, as he begins to undergo his moral redemption, Pip realises his misjudgement and begins to establish an affectionate, fulfilling relationship with his benefactor. Finally, through Magwitch's death, Dickens provides an overt opportunity for Pip to display his newfound loyalty and moral integrity, visiting Magwitch in prison every day towards the end of his life and confiding in him. Dickens ultimately portrays the **value of genuine human connection to be immensely more fulfilling than wealth and status.**

Joe Gargery

Joe Gargery is Pip's brother-in-law who emblematises the proletarian life that Pip aspires to escape, yet inevitably learns to value. Exemplifying the honourable values of the working-class, Joe's morally righteous filial relationship with Pip is one of comfort and satisfaction and further commends Joe's working-class fulfilment from his physical labour.

Unaffected by the influence of the upper-class society, **Joe remains virtuous and constantly supportive** throughout Pip's journey to becoming a gentleman. This is all despite the emerging shame and resentment that Pip expresses towards Joe's coarse appearance and lack of education, wishing that he "had been more genteelly brought up" to fit in with the standards of the bourgeoise society. Unlike the other characters, such as Mrs Joe, Mr Pumblechook, and even Pip, Joe disregards the seemingly natural desire to "increase [his] income" to gain economic superiority, or to make "theatrical declamations" from a pretentious façade to gain moral superiority.

Instead, Joe becomes an exception to the impressionable and perpetually dissatisfied middle-class and upper-class characters, illustrated by Dickens through his fair treatment of those 'below' him, referring to Magwitch as a "poor fellow, creature." This contributes to Dickens' depiction of the **arbitrary nature of class hierarchy when compared to the genuine value of emotional connection and loyalty.** Joe's unwavering tenderness towards Pip throughout all the stages of Pip's life demonstrates the kind-heartedness of Joe's character. As a result of this, he is rewarded with happiness and satisfaction at the conclusion of the novel, marrying Biddy and being content with his occupation as a blacksmith.

Mrs Joe

Mrs Joe is Pip's sister. She is only known under her marital title of Mrs Joe Gargery throughout the novel; she is never granted a first name (reflective of the role of the wife in Victorian society). She is a strict and severe woman that has been condemned to a working-class life that she is ultimately dissatisfied with. However, like many other characters in the novel she wishes to be more upper-class than she is. Because of this she constructs a façade in the presence of company above her in the social hierarchy, such as Mr Pumblechook and Mr Wopsle.

In the eyes of Pip, Mrs Joe is a cruel woman renowned for her furious rampages and punishments, disciplining both Joe and Pip until her fatal attack at the hands of Orlick. The attack softens her demeanour, exposing a certain helplessness in her character. The death of Mrs Joe serves as a significant marker of Pip's maturation, as despite having left behind his working-class life on the forge, the death of his sister affects him more deeply than he expected, displaying the continual reminders of his past life that haunt his morally corrupted ascent to affluence and status.

Biddy

Biddy, being Mr Wopsle's great-aunt's granddaughter, plays a multifaceted role throughout *Great Expectations* as Pip's teacher, friend, voice of reason, and **contrasting love interest to Estella.** As such, throughout the narrative, Biddy's character is used as a reflection of Pip's constantly evolving worldview, yet she consistently upholds the same honourable, proletarian values of authenticity and empathy representing the comfort and fulfilment of the working-class life that Pip endeavours to escape.

Initially, seeking Biddy's education and companionship, Pip admires Biddy's knowledge and support. Yet in achieving his great expectations and becoming accustomed to the capitalistic etiquette and ideals of the upper-class, Pip begins to condescend Biddy which is juxtaposed with her kind-hearted nature.

Nonetheless, throughout Pip's failed romantic aspirations to win Estella's affection, he repeatedly acknowledges the satisfaction that he could have achieved through a humble, honest life married to Biddy who would never manipulate or taunt Pip with the cruel intentions that Estella does. At the end of the novel, Biddy receives a happy fate, marrying Joe and having two children, suggesting that on some level Dickens is endorsing her worldview as a more righteous one for readers to aspire to.

Mr Jaggers

Mr Jaggers is the powerful and influential lawyer hired by Magwitch to be Pip's guardian in his journey towards becoming a gentleman. As such, **Jaggers embodies the capitalist attitudes of the upper class,** in which the concept of justice is obscured by a prevailing prioritisation of economic gain over genuine fairness.

Although Jaggers is meant to be a guardian figure for Pip, Dickens portrays Jaggers' attitude as being one of contractual obligation based purely on the materialistic incentive that Jaggers is paid to fulfil a service. This stands in stark contrast to Pip's filial camaraderie with Joe. Through this juxtaposition, Dickens exhibits the **lack of fulfilment gained from the transactional relationships of the meretricious upper class** in contrast to the **satisfaction derived from genuine human connection**, which Pip experiences in his proletarian life. As Pip substitutes his companionship with Joe for the economically based guardianship of Mr Jaggers, Dickens is able to delineate the subsequent shifts that occur in Pip's moral values.

However, whilst Jaggers is depicted as an unrivalled figure of strength and power, Dickens gives dimension to his character by divulging Jaggers' generosity, softness, and even hints of insecurity in his contributions to helping young Estella to find a home with Miss Havisham in order to save her from leading a life of crime similar to that of her biological mother. An important motif in Jaggers' character is the **obsessive washing of his hands after working with his criminal clients.** This suggests a certain necessity felt by Jaggers to **avoid the ethical implications of his work,** as a lawyer defending his criminal clients, from tainting the morality of his personal life.

Herbert Pocket

Similarly to Joe, **Herbert demonstrates the honourable values of loyalty and friendship,** prioritising his relationship with Pip over the corrupted, materialistic values of the upper class. As such, Dickens often **juxtaposes Herbert's virtuousness and generosity to the increasing self-centredness and arrogance of Pip** who is blinded by his ambitions for wealth and status. Ultimately, Herbert is portrayed by Dickens as an authentic exemplar of companionship, standing by Pip throughout his rise and fall in prospects and subsequently being rewarded with contentment in his job and marriage to his beloved Clara.

Wemmick

John Wemmick, known predominately as just Wemmick throughout the novel, is Mr Jaggers' clerk who strikes up an authentic friendship with Pip. He is portrayed by Dickens as a **peculiar man with a distinct separation between his work life and personal life.** Whilst at work, Wemmick is the cynical and stern embodiment of economically driven values, persistently lecturing Pip about the importance of "portable property," yet it turns out that this seriousness is a façade when contrasted to his jovial, good-humoured, and tender nature when existing at his home in Walworth.

Wemmick cheerfully takes pride in his wholesome, self-made "little wooden cottage in the midst of plots of garden" and enjoys a fulfilling private life of gardening and caring for his "aged parent." Thus, Wemmick's character becomes congruent with Dickens' suggestion that **in order to seek genuine satisfaction in the upper class of a capitalist society, it is necessary to adopt external, public façades that differentiate the occupational and personal lives of an individual.**

Dolge Orlick

Dolge Orlick is the "morose journeyman" that works as a day labourer in Joe's forge and is depicted by Dickens as a truly evil character. Dickens establishes the **character of Orlick to be an amoral figure of malice, deriving joy from the suffering of others.** This is evidenced by his physical attributes being a "loose limbed swarthy fellow [...] always slouching" as well as the unsettlingly gluttonous and grotesque sound of his name.

His villainous nature haunts Pip throughout the novel as Orlick is responsible for Mrs Joe's attack and subsequent death, as well as attempting to murder Pip later in the narrative out of his own irrational jealousy and resentment. Whilst Dickens questions the objectivity of good and bad throughout *Great Expectations*, Orlick is **one of the few characters that embodies pure malevolence.**

Compeyson

Compeyson is another criminal and convict who prior to the beginning of the novel was a partner of Magwitch. Compeyson is described by Dickens to be an **educated gentleman invested in a criminal career** of "swindling, handwriting forging, [and] stolen bank-note passing" who manipulated control over Magwitch in their shared crimes resulting in the arrest of both men. As the narrative progresses, various revelations lead reader to realise that he is the man who betrayed Miss Havisham, breaking her heart on their wedding day. He is also found to be responsible for the capture of Magwitch towards the latter part of the narrative.

As a result of his upper-class upbringing, Compeyson's more generous treatment in court is used by Dickens to **highlight the biases of the legal system in 19th century England,** favouring those who align with the values and appearances of the capitalistic bourgeoisie over those from working class origins, regardless of the severity of their crime.

Dickens condemns how this serves to perpetuate and validate the **social class divide**, operating under the prejudices of the **Victorian societal superstructure.** This is evinced through Magwitch's frustrations that Compeyson, a well-dressed, "well brought up" gentleman is treated with a respectable sense of justice, receiving a sentence of only seven years despite having been the mastermind behind the crime. This is compared to Magwitch, "the elder, ill brought up" accomplice, who did not have the advantages of being an educated gentleman and so received a fourteen-year sentence.

Uncle Pumblechook

Mr Pumblechook, also known as Uncle Pumblechook (being Pip's uncle-in-law) is a **pompous and entitled middle-class man,** obsessed with prospects of wealth and social superiority. He is constantly characterised by his arrogance, egotistical nature, and the "chaise-cart" which he flaunts as a symbol of his prestige and meretricious affluence. Mr Pumblechook also persistently takes credit for Pip's rise in fortune and status despite only being responsible for arranging Pip's initial invitation to Satis House.

In the presence of others, Pumblechook claims to be the originator of Pip's handsome inheritance despite having absolutely no connection to Magwitch, the source of Pip's great expectations. As such, Pumblechook **represents the prevailing entitlement of the burgeoning bourgeoise class** and the ultimately futile value attributed to displays of material wealth in a capitalist society.

Bentley Drummle

Bentley Drummle is an unpleasant young man, heir to a baronetcy, who Pip encounters whilst being tutored at the Pockets' House. He is depicted by Dickens as a **detestable brute and exhibits a prevailing sense of arrogance and superiority** which causes him to patronise Pip and the other characters around him.

Drummle frustrates Pip throughout the novel as he invalidates Pip's understanding of how one can attain status. Pip believes that one must have education, morality, money, and social connections to attain status in the upper-class hierarchy. Yet Drummle, neither well educated or morally righteous, is a well-respected and influent figure. Dickens thus **highlights the hypocrisies and deceptions rife in the class system which favours aristocracy and generational wealth over all other attributes.** While Pip believes that with enough education, good manners, and appropriate dress he can be a gentleman, Drummle shows him the true and ugly side of the upper class – that your origins will always impact on your prospects in society.

Minor characters

Startop

Startop is a loyal friend of Pip who is also tutored by Mr Matthew Pocket. He is an intelligent and kind young man who eventually assists Pip and Herbert in their scheme for Magwitch's escape demonstrating loyalty and friendship.

Mr Wopsle

Mr Wopsle is the church clerk in Pip's village who moves to London in pursuit of becoming an actor. This provides an ironic similarity between Wopsle's elaborate caricature-like performances of characters in a play and Pip's superficial façade of becoming a gentleman.

Mr Wopsle's great-aunt

She is the incompetent and slothful teacher at the village evening school which Pip attends in his youth. Her lazy manner of educating differs greatly to the upper-class education of social etiquette and bourgeois ideals that Pip receives in his hierarchical ascent.

Matthew Pocket

Matthew Pocket, also referred to as Mr Pocket, is Herbert's father, Miss Havisham's cousin, and Pip's tutor. He is an intelligent man yet is incompetent in controlling his home life with his wife and many children. Throughout the narrative he is kind to Pip and Pip repays this kindness by commending Matthew Pocket's support to Miss Havisham, resulting in her leaving a sum of money to him in her will.

Mrs Pocket

Mrs Pocket is Herbert's mother and embodies the typical figure of a bourgeoise wife. She ignores her maternal duties, allowing her servants to run the household and raise her children whilst she spends her time dwelling on her distant noble lineage and thinking about the prestige of upper-class society life.

Molly

Molly is a reformed criminal who becomes Mr Jaggers' housekeeper and is eventually revealed to be Estella's biological mother. Through the revelation of Molly being Estella's mother (and Magwitch being her father), Dickens uproots Pip's simplistic understanding of social class, challenging his acquired, rigid bourgeoisie perceptions that being born of low origins is shameful and implies a sense of impurity.

Arthur Havisham

Arthur is Miss Havisham's resentful half-brother who became a partner to Compeyson, contributing to the scheme that betrayed her on her wedding day.

Section 5
Key Themes Analysis

Social class

Throughout the novel, the exploration of social class and hierarchy is a central theme that contextualises Dickens' narrative in the rigidly structured social climate of Victorian England. Through the development of a range of complex characters that occupy various places in the social hierarchy, such as criminals like Magwitch, working-class individuals like Joe and Biddy, rapacious middle-class members such as Mr Pumblechook, and affluent characters like Miss Havisham, Dickens explores and questions the integrity and value of these strict parameters of societal value.

At the beginning of the novel, Pip is sheltered by his working-class upbringing on the marshes with Joe who is an exemplary embodiment of the honest, kind-hearted proletarian figure. As an innocent young boy, Pip is entirely unaware of his low status and the implications of not having an upper-class upbringing. It is only when Pip ventures out of his home on the marshes to visit Satis House that he is confronted with the shame and humiliation associated with his hierarchical position. From this point on, Pip becomes hyper-aware of his place in society and subsequently his desire to become a gentleman arises, fuelled by his perpetual dissatisfaction with his present status.

After receiving his "handsome fortune" and becoming a gentleman, one would think that Pip would be satisfied with his rise in status. However, having a proletarian upbringing, he becomes somewhat alienated from the bourgeoisie as he does not have the classical education and etiquette of a "true gentleman," yet he is also simultaneously alienated from the working class as he no longer has a connection to any kind of physical labour. As the plot evolves, Dickens purports that wealth and status are far less valuable than affection, loyalty, and kind-heartedness, ultimately questioning the integrity and merit of the merciless 19th century societal structure.

Throughout his rise and fall from high society, **Pip learns that one's social class is not indicative of their genuine value.** For example, the upper-class Bentley Drummle is revealed to be an insufferable, violent brute, whilst Magwitch, a lowly convict, turns out to possess a profound inner value and moral compass. Even more so, Joe, a working-class blacksmith, is seen to epitomise the value of genuine human relationships over the prestige of money and status.

Furthermore, through various revelations in the narrative, such as the discovery of Estella's parentage and the interconnections between the seemingly separate worlds of Magwitch and Miss Havisham, Dickens questions the restriction of class mobility in Victorian society. In doing so, he uproots Pip's understanding of the value of social merit and thus further exhibits to the reader the prevailing resolution that ultimately **being a kind, generous, and loyal person has far more merit than acquiring wealth and power.**

Morality and ethics

Through the themes of morality and ethics, Dickens distinguishes between performative virtuousness and genuinely righteous morality. He also explores the rights and wrongs of crime, guilt, and innocence. The most prominent initial encounter that Pip has with the concept of morality is in chapter 4 when the family and Mrs Joe's friends gather for Christmas. As the guests boast of their moral superiority, lecturing Pip about gratitude and virtue, they only give him scraps to eat. Meanwhile, the virtuous Joe give Pip gravy from his plate in an act of kindness. Through this, Dickens reveals the theatrical façade of ethics and superiority adopted by these characters to seem more honourable and upper-class than they actually are.

Furthermore, Dickens contrasts this to the genuine good nature of Joe and Biddy who constantly stand by their authentic beliefs throughout the novel, even when Pip's sense of morality diminishes with his rise to fortune. Joe even selflessly nurses Pip back to health and pays off his debts despite Pip's horrible treatment of him.

Pip's journey to becoming a gentleman and subsequently his fall from wealth and high status is partially defined by a transformation of his moral compass. At the start of the novel, Pip is the embodiment of youthful innocence, yet his burgeoning ambition to ascend the social hierarchy comes at the expense of his virtue, replacing his values of camaraderie and affection with a rapacious and insatiable desire for material wealth and status. During this time, he becomes blind to his unethical treatment of those who he once cared for greatly. As the narrative progresses, **Pip becomes aware of his amoral attitudes and endeavours to repair his fractured relationships, regaining the moral integrity that he once had.**

The same themes are explored by Dickens through the lens of crime, guilt, punishment, and innocence. Characters like the convicts and Mr Jaggers facilitate an exploration into the complexities of morality and ethics. Imagery of crime and the legal system pervades the entirety of the narrative, from the handcuffs brought to be repaired by Joe at the beginning of the novel to the unpleasant interior of Newgate prison. This becomes **symbolic of Pip's internal conflict in reconciling his own understanding of moral conscience with the unjust external framework of institutional justice** which is portrayed by Dickens as supporting the meretricious values of the upper class.

Punishment is also used by Dickens to indicate the consequences of immoral and unjust actions. Mrs Joe, Miss Havisham, and Compeyson all meet horrible fates, either dying or getting brutally injured. Each of these characters act with cruelty, deceit, manipulation, or unkindness throughout the novel. Mrs Joe is cruel to both Pip and Joe, Miss Havisham evilly manipulates Pip throughout the novel for her own revenge and resigns Estella to a life of misery, and Compeyson was responsible for Miss Havisham's failed wedding and the attempted murder of Pip. Thus, **Dickens indicates that despite people's appearances or wealth, immoral actions will always have horrific consequences.**

Dickens also questions **the integrity of the criminal justice system** including the institutional bodies of the police, jails, and courts as prejudiced entities often **serving to validate the views of the upper class** rather than resolve conflict with morally just intentions. Magwitch is initially perceived by Pip as a frightening, barbaric figure due to his title as a convict, in response to this Pip is overcome by the guilt of assisting a criminal. Yet, as the narrative unfolds, Pip discovers Magwitch's inner generosity and nobility and eventually sees past the convict's external status as an unworthy criminal. Eventually, with his reformed moral conscience, Pip further assists Magwitch in evading the law by attempting to help him escape London. Through this journey of shifts in morality, **Pip ascertains that the only valuable judgement is the assessment of one's true character, kind-hearted intentions, and authenticity** rather than what society has labelled them or their external appearance.

Ambition

The theme of ambition drives the narrative of *Great Expectations*, displaying both the positive and negative consequences of Pip's pursuits throughout the novel. Pip's confrontation with the shame associated with his working-class status and subsequent desires to become worthy of Estella's attention stokes his ambition and his pursuit to become a gentleman. However, Dickens elucidates the insatiable nature of this ambition as **Pip is never truly satisfied with attaining an upper-class life,** despite gaining a large fortune and a gentleman's education. Furthermore, Pip's achievement of his great expectations is critiqued by Dickens as being undeniably pyrrhic, as Pip's moral compass and his relationships with the honourable characters of Joe and Biddy are damaged.

Pip's ambition facilitates his hierarchical ascent, yet is also the reason for his downfall, as Dickens delineates his burgeoning arrogance and self-centredness as synonymous with his merciless yearning for wealth and status. This hunger to achieve a life of upper-class privilege leaves Pip in a state of perpetual dissatisfaction, becoming lonely and frustrated, never winning the true object of his desires, Estella.

After all of his expectations begin to dissolve, Pip's ambition is inherently what drives his redemption. Instead of yearning for material value and hierarchical superiority, Pip finally learns the true path to satisfaction through genuine affection and honest work, with his ambition fuelling his journey to self-improvement. Pip concludes the novel with a newfound perspective of maturity achieved as a result of his endeavours to redeem himself.

Etiquette

Throughout the novel, Dickens explores the societal norms and expectations that govern 19th century English society and articulates the consequences of adhering to and deviating from these standards. As such, social etiquette and the pursuit of sophistication significantly shape the lives of Dickens' characters across the vast expanse of their individual hierarchical positions.

Initially, Pip's introduction to the pursuit of sophistication comes from his sister's endeavours to appear more upper-class in the presence of guests. Dickens conveys a sense of artifice in his depiction of Mrs Joe setting out to dine in the parlour, changing the curtains, and adopting a generally more pleasant demeanour in the company of her guests at the Christmas dinner early in the novel. It is through Mrs Joe's dissatisfaction with her impoverished lifestyle and her consequent attempts to align with the expectations of her middle-class guests that Dickens establishes an **association between the arbitrary acts of 'sophistication' and the irrational values of the upper class.**

Furthermore, a fundamental challenge that Pip faces during his journey to become a gentleman is his lack of knowledge on etiquette and the significant value attributed to these manners in bourgeoisie society. This becomes most evident when Pip dines at Barnard's Inn with Herbert Pocket for the first time and is entirely unaccustomed to the intricate manners expected of a gentleman whilst eating. Herbert corrects Pip, articulating that "the spoon is not generally used over-hand, but under" and that "society as a body does not expect one to be so strictly conscientious in emptying one's glass, as to turn it bottom upwards with the rim on one's nose." In expressing these mannerisms, that differ greatly to the unregulated dining of Pip's life on the marshes and even more drastically to the "dog-like" manners of Magwitch earlier in the novel, Dickens exhibits the bourgeoise tendencies to **prioritise displays of etiquette and leisure over instinctual or essential acts of survival.**

Nonetheless, these arbitrary mannerisms are substantiated and somewhat validated by characters in the novel, disguising the genuine reasoning for these displays of superiority with seemingly logical explanations to "get at your mouth better" or to avoid "accidents." Dickens reveals that rather than being indicators of classical education and esteemed knowledge, these **performative exhibitions of etiquette create and validate the disjunction between the upper and lower social classes. Dickens thus exposes the superficiality of a society that places excessive value on outward appearances** and criticises characters, like Drummle, Compeyson, and Pumblechook, that embody the snobbish and capitalistic etiquette of the upper class whilst fundamentally upholding immoral values.

Loyalty, friendship, and genuine human relationships

In essence, Charles Dickens' *Great Expectations* **is a story about the importance of loyalty, friendship, and genuine human connection over hollow pursuits of fortune and social standing.** Throughout the novel, Dickens explores the profound value of loyalty, friendship, and genuine human connection in contrast to the capitalistic attitudes of self-centredness and arrogance portrayed by the upper class, ultimately imparting that **true satisfaction can only be achieved through authentic, fulfilling relationships.**

Loyalty is a prevailing theme that defines the genuine relationships of *Great Expectations*, the most notable being Pip's filial camaraderie with his brother-in-law Joe Gargery. Joe and Pip's relationship, preceding Pip's rise in fortune and valuing of pretentious upper-class societal expectations, is depicted by Dickens as a satisfying bond of selflessness and affection. Joe is an embodiment of the virtuous attributes of honesty and kindness, and his unwavering support and care for Pip from his childhood to his destitution towards the latter stages of the novel demonstrate the kind-heartedness of his character. Dickens thus rewards Joe with happiness and satisfaction at the conclusion of the novel, as Joe marries Biddy and carries on living his contented life.

Similarly, the theme of friendship arises with the introduction of Herbert Pocket who forms an **immutable companionship with Pip as they navigate the trials and tribulations of the upper-class world together.** Despite financial challenges and Pip's self-serving desire for hierarchical ascension, Herbert remains loyal to Pip, even saving his life after an almost fatal encounter with the malicious Orlick. In conveying their affectionate bond, Dickens illuminates the **integrity of true friendships and the positive influences of genuine companionship.**

Towards the end of the novel Pip creates a genuine filial connection with his benefactor Magwitch. This evolving relationship, in congruence with his authentic generosity in providing Pip with a "handsome fortune," further strengthens Dickens' suggestion that **one's value can only be determined by the righteousness of their actions and intentions, rather than their external appearance or prescribed societal role.**

Dickens also explores relationships that are completely antithetical to loyalty and fulfilment through characters such as Miss Havisham, who is depicted to be the epitome of resentment and heartlessness. After indulging in a disturbing life of malevolent manipulation, it is only when she meets her tragic fate that she realises her wrongdoings and seeks forgiveness, ultimately discovering the value of empathy and kindness when it is too late to repair the damage she had caused. Thus, Dickens portrays **authentic relationships with trust and loyalty as the only way to live a satisfying and fulfilling life.** Miss Havisham, Orlick, and Compeyson are met with an awful end, yet Herbert, Wemmick, Joe, and Biddy all experience happiness and fulfilment with loving marriages and gratifying work – a testament to their moral attitudes towards friendship and loyalty.

Manipulation

In *Great Expectations*, Dickens lays bare the deceitful nature of the upper classes and consequently shows how deceit can negatively impact those around them. To some extent, most of the characters in upper-class society operate under some kind of façade. Even Pip himself, once embroiled in the life of a gentlemen, manipulates others and operates with secrecy.

Miss Havisham is the most manipulative character in the novel, having adopted Estella with the purpose of getting revenge on men. Thus, she raises her as a tool, controlling Estella and others around her to suit her vicious game. Pip is the unfortunate test dummy for this cruelty, falling in love with Estella as a child exactly as Miss Havisham desired. Pip's heart is later broken by Estella, and Miss Havisham relishes in her victory. However, by the end of the novel Miss Havisham is horribly burnt and eventually dies, thus **Dickens purports that cruel and immoral acts of manipulation will invariably lead to suffering and destruction.**

In the process of getting her revenge on men, Miss Havisham ruins Estella's life, treating her as an object and instilling a lack of empathy and emotions in her, so by the end of the novel Estella is separated from her husband and "leading a most unhappy life." Pip similarly has come to misfortune, owing a great debt to Joe and losing his high-class status. Dickens uses these two characters to portray the effects of manipulation and duplicity on one's life and character; however, by the end of the novel both show remorse, so there is optimism in the concluding chapter for their futures. On the other hand, characters such as Joe and Biddy are given a clear happy and fulfilling ending, depicting the rewards of honesty and kindness. **As such, Dickens suggests that manipulation can lead to unhappiness and ruin, the only antidote to which is honesty, genuine companionship, and contentedness with one's path in life.**

Desire and objectification

Desire is much like ambition in the novel, as it is one of Pip's driving forces and also reinforces his conceited and over-confident nature. His desire for Estella and his irrational self-assurance bring Pip to his own misery but also serve to further Estella's objectification throughout the novel. To Pip, Estella is another accomplishment on his road to true high-society life. Like acquiring a fortune and learning manners, Pip assumes Estella is meant for him, reducing her agency and freedom just as Miss Havisham does throughout the novel.

Estella has been brought up as Miss Havisham's "Jewel," an object in her collection to take her revenge on men. By both Miss Havisham and Pip, she is seen only for her beauty and so Estella also sees herself this way. She acts exactly as she has been made to, cruelly and callously using her beauty to reject men and cause them pain and dissatisfaction. This leads to her unhappiness, marrying the brutish Bentley Drummle. However, in marrying Drummle Estella asserts her own agency for the first time, going against Miss Havisham's and Pip's wishes and marrying him anyway. Although it does not turn out positively, by the end of the novel she seems changed and can express her emotions to Pip, leaving the reader with a sense of positivity about her future.

Pip also objectifies Biddy, using her as a source of knowledge and comfort. Although he does admit she would make a wonderful wife and give him a happy life, he ultimately chooses to use her for his own ends to become a gentleman. At the end of the novel, Pip decides Biddy would be a perfect match for him and goes to marry her, but she is already happily married to Joe. Alternately, Joe sees the goodness in everyone, never approaching anyone with the purpose of furthering his own goals. Thus, he is rewarded with a happy and fulfilling life by the completion of the novel. The objectification of women then is seen as an **undesirable consequence of the rapacious greed and immoral manipulation required to participate in upper-class society,** which can only be overcome with the institution of genuine actions, sincere emotion, and agency.

Section 6
Structural Features Analysis

Great Expectations is considered a **bildungsroman** which is essentially a fancy word meaning that the **narrative follows the development of one main protagonist in their formative years as they grapple with their moral, psychological, and physical growth.** Divided into three volumes contained within the one novel, *Great Expectations* is set out chronologically to follow Pip's upbringing and education, rise to fortune, and subsequent loss of fortune and moral redemption.

Symbolism

Darkness and light

Omnipresent: something present everywhere all at once.

Chiaroscuro: the balance of light and dark shadows in a painting or artwork.

Dickens employs the **symbol of omnipresent darkness** throughout the novel, often serving as a **manifestation of Pip's uncertainty** as well as a **foreboding symbol of immorality.** Considering the significant presence of darkness in the story, the glimpses of light that arise create a **chiaroscuro** effect of shadow and light, often serving to **contrast moments of clarity and hope.**

For example, the persisting symbol of darkness is recursively employed by Dickens to emulate the uncertain and threatening nature in which Magwitch approaches Pip on the ominous, stormy night in London when he reveals his identity. The darkened physical environment, resulting from a blackout caused by the raging storm, immediately establishes a foreboding atmosphere and thus reflects the uncertainty felt by Pip towards the identity of his benefactor. Using only the "very contracted [...] circle of light" from his lamp to illuminate the stairwell in attempt to identify the approaching figure of Magwitch, Pip sees mere fragments of the convict as he ascends the staircase. Through this image of the minimal and constricted presence of light, Dickens **metaphorically portrays the restricted view of Pip to emulate his closed-mindedness and narrow worldview** due to his acquired self-centredness and bourgeoisie values. This darkness is also used throughout the novel to foreshadow Magwitch's appearance with the first time they meet occurring on a dark and gloomy afternoon and the weather darkening again when Magwitch returns to London.

Darkness and light are also used extensively in Satis House to instil in the reader a sense of melancholy and deception. The hallways of Satis House are oppressive and stifling as Miss Havisham sits in the mouldy darkness in her decaying home. This is contrasted against the warmth and light that Pip associates with the kitchen he shares with Joe in his small home.

The darkness of Satis House symbolises the oppressive nature of upper-class society and the objectification of high society ladies while the light in Joe's forge represents the happiness and contentedness that comes with an honest and humble life. As we learn of Miss Havisham's manipulations and cruel immoral behaviour, the darkness of Satis House can also be associated with immorality, symbolising her corruption under the influence of the duplicitous standards of bourgeoisie society.

In the final chapters, the fire that overcomes Miss Havisham lights up the once dark and depressing room after her apology to Pip. Fire is typically symbolic of purification; however, in this instance it enacts a sort of divine punishment for her actions throughout the novel. But in some ways it acts as a purification for the house, which is disassembled and sold off to potentially become something new. Whilst the fire ultimately kills Miss Havisham by the end of the novel, it also marks the realisation of her manipulative endeavours and ignites (pardon the pun) her desperate desires for forgiveness.

The weather and physical environment

Dickens repeatedly uses the weather and physical atmosphere in moments of the narrative to **foreshadow and reflect the emotions and actions of the characters.** For example, the turbulent storm that occurs right before Magwitch arrives to reveal his identity to Pip **symbolises the foreboding sense of turbulence and turmoil** that awaits Pip following the revelation of his benefactor's identity.

Equally, the peaceful, clear skies upon the marshes as Pip returns to the forge with the intention of repairing his relationships with Joe and Biddy reflects the clarity of Pip's intentions. He travels from the claustrophobic, polluted skies of London where he was plagued by internal conflict and loneliness to the picturesque natural landscape of his childhood home where he reconciles his relationship with his loved ones.

Another example of this is the **imagery of the mists over the marshes** which are illustrated by Dickens to **symbolise various moments of ambiguity,** the most prominent of which is the very last passage of the novel in which the "evening mists [rise]" after Pip's reunion with Estella. This could suggest either the clarity of the pair's resolution as "friends" or the potential for an optimistic future between them.

Time

Time is another recurring symbol in the novel which is most prevalent in the "transfixed" nature of time within Satis House. Miss Havisham's wealth affords her the **privilege of ignoring the reality of time** which the working class relies upon, explicitly evident in her quote "I know nothing of the days of the week; I know nothing of the weeks of the year." Miss Havisham can afford to ignore this seemingly vital concept of time, instead spending her days indulging in her manipulative games. However, this symbol of stopping time within Satis House also serves **to emphasise the inability for Miss Havisham to heal or evolve, ultimately resulting in her demise.**

This starkly contrasts the working-class characters in the novel, whose lives are dictated by the critical construct of time. Joe's physical labour adheres to the standard hours of the working week, emphasised by Pip's request for a "half-holiday" to visit Miss Havisham being contemplated by Joe and contested by Orlick. It is also evident in Pip's recounting of the difficulty of his education in the "winter season" when "one low spirited dip-candle" was the only light to illuminate the class. The effects of time then, whether it be the rising and setting of the sun or the passing of years, has a significant capacity to effect the upper and lower classes to different degrees.

Estella and the jewels

Throughout the novel, Estella is constantly reduced to a mere symbol of beauty and wealth. Devoid of any individual identity or autonomy, Estella is constantly being objectified as a "pawn" in Miss Havisham's malevolent games of manipulation and only acts on the demands of her adoptive mother. This is an overt symbol throughout the narrative as Pip expresses his romantic desires for Estella which becomes synonymous with his insatiable yearning for hierarchical ascension.

Miss Havisham flaunts Estella's beauty by displaying elegant arrays of expensive jewellery upon her, simultaneously enhancing Estella's beauty by associating it with the opulent material value of the jewels and enhancing the material value of the jewels by equating them with Estella's beauty. Estella herself becomes an object, like the jewels she wears, as if she is just one more jewel in Miss Havisham's collection. Thus, the **jewels symbolise her lack of identity and autonomy.** Ultimately, **Estella serves as the objectification achieved by affluence and elegance,** two interconnected qualities that drive Pip's ambition throughout the narrative, yet inevitably result in the debilitating objectification of Estella herself.

The "dog-like" simile

A repeated symbol that Dickens uses throughout the narrative is equating those of a lower status with a dog. This first appears in Pip's encounter with Magwitch on the marshes when he brings him "wittles" to eat. This dog-like manner of eating **represents the purely instinctual and survival-driven nature of eating in the lower classes.** This is in contrast to that of the upper classes who eat for leisure. This creates a shocking effect when applied to Pip upon his first visit to Satis House when Estella puts food on the ground for him to eat like a dog. This is when Pip first begins to realise his own low status and the shame associated with it. Ultimately, this is employed by Dickens to **emphasise the notion that there is always someone lower on the social hierarchy** than any given character at any given moment. It also accentuates the drastic differences in etiquette between the manner of eating in the upper and lower classes.

Section 7

Quote Bank

Social class

Quote	Character	Chapter
"A fearful man, all in coarse grey, with a great iron on his leg. A man with no hat, and with broken shoes, and with an old rag tied round his head. A man who had been soaked in water, and smothered in mud, and lamed by stones, and cut by flints, and stung by nettles, and torn by briars; who limped, and shivered, and glared, and growled."	Pip	1
"In his working clothes, Joe was a well-knit characteristic-looking blacksmith; in his holiday clothes, he was more like a scarecrow in good circumstances, than anything else. Nothing that he wore then, fitted him or seemed to belong to him; and everything that he wore then grazed him."	Pip	4
"I had heard of Miss Havisham up town – everybody for miles round, had heard of Miss Havisham up town – as an immensely rich and grim lady who lived in a large and dismal house barricaded against robbers, and who led a life of seclusion."	Pip	7
"I wished Joe had been rather more genteelly brought up, and then I should have been so too."	Pip	8
"I was a common labouring-boy; that my hands were coarse; that my boots were thick; that I had fallen into a despicable habit of calling knaves Jacks; that I was much more ignorant than I had considered myself last night, and generally that I was in a low-lived bad way."	Pip	8
"I had never thought of being ashamed of my hands before; but I began to consider them a very indifferent pair. Her contempt for me was so strong, that it became infectious, and I caught it."	Pip	8
"I took the opportunity of being alone in the courtyard, to look at my coarse hands and my common boots."	Pip	8

Quote	Speaker	Page
"I thought how Joe and my sister were then sitting in a kitchen, and how Miss Havisham and Estella never sat in a kitchen, but were far above the level of such common doings."	Pip	9
"Whatever I acquired, I tried to impart to Joe. This statement sounds so well, that I can't in my conscience let it pass unexplained. I wanted to make Joe less ignorant and common, that he might be worthier of my society and less open to Estella's reproach."	Pip	15
"'Biddy,' said I, after binding her to secrecy, 'I want to be a gentleman.'"	Pip	17
"And now, because my mind was not confused enough before, I complicated its confusion fifty thousand-fold, by having states and seasons when I was clear that Biddy was immeasurably better than Estella, and that the plain honest working life to which I was born, had nothing in it to be ashamed of, but offered me sufficient means of self-respect and happiness."	Pip	17
"It is considered that you must be better educated, in accordance with your altered position, and that you will be alive to the importance and necessity of at once entering on that advantage."	Mr Jaggers	18
"Her father was a country gentleman down in your part of the world, and was a brewer. I don't know why it should be a crack thing to be a brewer; but it is indisputable that while you can't possibly be genteel and bake, you may be as genteel as never was and brew. You see it every day."	Herbert Pocket	22

Morality and ethics

Quote	Character	Chapter
"I got so smartingly touched up by these moral goads."	Pip	4
"I was always treated as if I had insisted on being born, in opposition to the dictates of reason, religion, and morality,"	Pip	4
"'Trouble?' echoed my sister; 'trouble?' And then entered on a fearful catalogue of all the illnesses I had been guilty of, and all the acts of sleeplessness I had committed, and all the high places I had tumbled from, and all the low places I had tumbled into, and all the injuries I had done myself, and all the times she had wished me in my grave, and I had contumaciously refused to go there."	Pip	4
"I am what you have made me. Take all the praise, take all the blame; take all the success, take all the failure"	Estella	38
"'I want,' she said, 'to pursue that subject you mentioned to me when you were last here, and to show you that I am not all stone. But perhaps you can never believe, now, that there is anything human in my heart?'"	Miss Havisham	49
"There was a long hard time when I kept far from me the remembrance of what I had thrown away when I was quite ignorant of its worth."	Pip	59

Ambition

Quote	Character	Chapter
"The felicitous idea occurred to me a morning or two later when I woke, that the best step I could take towards making myself uncommon was to get out of Biddy everything she knew."	Pip	10
"I had believed in the forge as the glowing road to manhood and independence. Within a single year all this was changed."	Pip	14
"I wanted to make Joe less ignorant and common, that he might be worthier of my society and less open to Estella's reproach"	Pip	15

Quote	Character	Chapter
"my desire to be wiser"	Pip	15
"'Biddy,' said I, after binding her to secrecy, 'I want to be a gentleman.' 'Oh, I wouldn't, if I was you!' she returned. 'I don't think it would answer.' 'Biddy,' said I, with some severity, 'I have particular reasons for wanting to be a gentleman.'"	Pip	17
"Truly it was impossible to dissociate her presence from all those wretched hankerings after money and gentility that had disturbed my boyhood – from all those ill-regulated aspirations that had first made me ashamed of home and Joe"	Pip	29

Etiquette

Quote	Character	Chapter
"He was already handing mincemeat down his throat in the most curious manner, more like a man who was putting it away somewhere in a violent hurry, than a man who was eating it"	Pip	3
"I had often watched a large dog of ours eating his food; and I now noticed a decided similarity between the dog's way of eating, and the man's."	Pip	3
"In the meantime, Mrs Joe put clean white curtains up, and tacked a new flowered flounce across the wide chimney to replace the old one, and uncovered the little state parlour across the passage, which was never uncovered at any other time"	Pip	4
"the spoon is not generally used over-hand, but under"	Herbert	22
"society as a body does not expect one to be so strictly conscientious in emptying one's glass, as to turn it bottom upwards with the rim on one's nose."	Herbert	22

Loyalty, friendship, and genuine human relationships

Quote	Character	Chapter
"In our already-mentioned freemasonry as fellow-sufferers, and in his good-natured companionship with me, it was our evening habit to compare the way we bit through our slices, by silently holding them up to each other's admiration now and then, which stimulated us to new exertions."	Pip	2
"'When I offered to your sister to keep company, and to be asked in church at such times as she was willing and ready to come to the forge, I said to her, "And bring the poor little child. God bless the poor little child," I said to your sister, "there's room for him at the forge!"'"	Joe Gargery	7
"O dear good Joe, whom I was so ready to leave and so unthankful to, I see you again, with your muscular blacksmith's arm before your eyes, and your broad chest heaving, and your voice dying away. O dear good faithful tender Joe, I feel the loving tremble of your hand upon my arm, as solemnly this day as if it had been the rustle of an angel's wing!"	Pip	18
"Herbert Pocket had a frank and easy way with him that was very taking. I had never seen any one then, and I have never seen any one since, who more strongly expressed to me, in every look and tone, a natural incapacity to do anything secret and mean."	Pip	22
"It was fine summer weather again, and, as I walked along, the times when I was a little helpless creature, and my sister did not spare me, vividly returned. But they returned with a gentle tone upon them that softened even the edge of Tickler. For now, the very breath of the beans and clover whispered to my heart that the day must come when it would be well for my memory that others walking in the sunshine should be softened as they thought of me."	Pip	35
"Look'ee here, Pip. I'm your second father. You're my son – more to me nor any son. I've put away money, only for you to spend."	Abel Magwitch	39
"Herbert received me with open arms, and I had never felt before, so blessedly, what it is to have a friend."	Pip	41

Quote	Character	Page
"Startop. A good fellow, a skilled hand, fond of us, and enthusiastic and honourable."	Herbert	52
"My mind, with inconceivable rapidity, followed out all the consequences of such a death. Estella's father would believe I had deserted him, would be taken, would die accusing me; even Herbert would doubt me, when he compared the letter I had left for him, with the fact that I had called at Miss Havisham's gate for only a moment; Joe and Biddy would never know how sorry I had been that night; none would ever know what I had suffered, how true I had meant to be, what an agony I had passed through."	Pip	53
"'But he knowed Orlick, and Orlick's in the county jail."	Joe	57
"O Joe, you break my heart! Look angry at me, Joe. Strike me, Joe. Tell me of my ingratitude. Don't be so good to me!"	Pip	57
"For, the tenderness of Joe was so beautifully proportioned to my need, that I was like a child in his hands."	Pip	57
"'Which dear old Pip, old chap,' said Joe, 'you and me was ever friends. And when you're well enough to go out for a ride – what larks!'"	Joe	57
"Ever the best of friends; ain't us, Pip?"	Joe	57
"Enclosed in the letter, was a receipt for the debt and costs on which I had been arrested. Down to that moment I had vainly supposed that my creditor had withdrawn or suspended proceedings until I should be quite recovered. I had never dreamed of Joe's having paid the money; but, Joe had paid it, and the receipt was in his name."	Pip	57
"I went towards them slowly [Joe and Biddy], leaving arrogance and untruthfulness further and further behind."	Pip	58
"They awakened a tender emotion in me; for my heart was softened by my return"	Pip	58

Manipulation, desire, and objectification

Quote	Character	Chapter
"Miss Havisham would often ask me in a whisper, or when we were alone, 'Does she grow prettier and prettier, Pip?' And when I said yes (for indeed she did), would seem to enjoy it greedily."	Pip	12
"I saw in this, that Estella was set to wreak Miss Havisham's revenge on men."	Pip	38
"Estella, with a sigh, as if she were tired; 'I am to write to her constantly and see her regularly and report how I go on – I and the jewels – for they are nearly all mine now.'"	Pip and Estella	33
"two cherry-coloured maids came fluttering out to receive Estella. The doorway soon absorbed her boxes."	Pip	33
"I saw in this, that I, too, was tormented by a perversion of ingenuity, even while the prize was reserved for me."	Pip	38
"I loved her against reason, against promise, against peace, against hope, against happiness, against all discouragement that could be."	Pip	29
"Love her, love her, love her! If she favours you, love her. If she wounds you, love her. If she tears your heart to pieces, and as it gets older and stronger it will tear deeper, love her, love her, love her!"	Miss Havisham	29
"I am what you have made me. Take all the praise, take all the blame; take all the success, take all the failure; in short, take me."	Estella	38
"Miss Havisham's intentions towards me, all a mere dream; Estella not designed for me; I only suffered in Satis House as a convenience, a sting for the greedy relations, a model with a mechanical heart to practise on when no other practice was at hand."	Pip	39
"Out of my thoughts! You are part of my existence, part of myself. You have been in every line I have ever read since I first came here, the rough common boy whose poor heart you wounded even then."	Pip	44

Section 8

Sample Essays

Essay One

QUESTION: To what extent does Victorian society influence characters and their relationships in *Great Expectations*?

ESSAY	COMMENTS
INTRODUCTION Through the novel *Great Expectations*, Charles Dickens criticises[1] the dominant influence of the rapacious and materialistic Victorian society[2] on his characters' identity and relationships. Dickens condemns the manner in which these arbitrary societal conventions corrupt genuine relationships, substituting them for transactional exchanges and amoral ethics. This is evident in Pip's social ascension which ignites change in his own identity, as well as his relationships with other characters such as Joe, Herbert, and Magwitch. Similarly, Miss Havisham and Estella's actions throughout the novel portray the effects of 19th century hierarchal society on women and those around them.	1. Notice how I haven't simply started my essay by restating the question? Whilst it is very important to make sure that you are answering the prompt, you will be able to make your writing more interesting by elaborating on the topics that the prompt suggests. 2. In describing the values of Victorian society in the introduction, I have given some important context to its role in *Great Expectations* rather than just its broad impacts on society.

PARAGRAPH 1

Joe and Pip's relationship, before Pip becomes obsessed with hierarchical advancement and economically biased ethics, is depicted by Dickens as one of honestly and integrity. However, through Pip's ambition to advance in society and become a gentleman, his relationship with Joe becomes warped and disingenuous as Pip begins to criticise and resent Joe and his humble upbringings. During Pip's introduction to high-society life, he becomes dissatisfied with his simple life and wishes Joe were "more genteelly brought up."[3] Similarly, he admonishes Biddy and even himself, finding fault in his clothes, shoes, and the way he calls "knaves Jacks." This change in his relationship with those around him is symbolic of the influence the rapacious upper-class society has on those who surrender to it.[4] Pip becomes embroiled in the life of a gentleman, rejecting his past life and genuine relationships in exchange for the duplicitous and manipulative exchanges of the upper-class. As such, he becomes buried in debt, is rejected by the cruel Estella, and is nearly killed by Orlick. Meanwhile, Joe, who stays true to his simple life and genuine human connections, marries Biddy and has two wonderful children. Thus, through the changing nature of Joe and Pip's relationship and their consequential endings, Dickens purports that the duplicitous and greedy lifestyle of the bourgeoisie can only lead to a miserable and unsatisfying life, while prioritising honesty and genuine relationships will lead to a life of fulfilment.[5]

3. Rather than using the full quote, you can use a small part of it to make your writing flow better yet still concisely make your point.

4. In writing an essay like this, it is important to both zoom in and zoom out. The notated section here is a good example of zooming out, essentially connecting your point back to the themes of the text and/or the prompt. Zooming out is generally looking at the overarching themes rather than the events that occur during the narrative.

5. Make sure to bring your argument back to the prompt to sum up your paragraph. In the introduction we have begun an argument of Dickens' stance on Victorian upper-class society and how he uses changing relationships to express this throughout the novel, thus we must back this point up throughout the essay.

PARAGRAPH 2

Pip's hierarchal ascent and descent throughout *Great Expectations* is used by Dickens to expose the damaging effects 19th century Victorian values can have on an individual, critiquing the ability of these values to subvert an individual's identity through corruption and immorality. At the beginning of the novel, Pip is depicted as an innocent, young, working-class boy who has a strong moral compass and heartfelt connections with those around him. However, once introduced to the values of the upper class at Satis House and being made aware of his "course hands" and "common boots," Pip is irreversibly corrupted to pursue only economic and social superiority over those around him.[6] In becoming aware of his "great expectations," Pip begins to value economic gain over genuine relationships as he accepts Mr Jaggers' contractual guardianship over his own emotional connection with Joe. Through alliteration and plosive sounds[7] in Mr Jaggers' speech informing Pip of his "expectations," Dickens hyperbolises the reduction of relationships to transactional exchanges. Pip's identity is thus completely warped by his introduction into this society. He is sculpted into the embodiment of the bourgeoisie, adopting arbitrary prejudices, capitalistic superiority, alienation from any form of meritocratic work, and a sense of perpetual dissatisfaction. Ultimately, it takes Pip's ascent and descent of the social hierarchy for him to be see the reality of class as a divisive social construct.[8]

6. Notice how these short, blended quotes enhance the analysis without interrupting the flow? This is an ideal way to demonstrate your in-depth knowledge of the text while still concentrating on your thesis and the progression of the essay.
7. Use literary techniques to back up your points where you can.
8. By the ends of your paragraphs, you should be ready to make an interpretive judgement like this to convey your reading of the text in relation to the prompt's focus. In this case, we're expanding on the idea of society influencing a character and saying that it's only after experiencing the vicissitudes of Victorian society that Pip truly understands the reality of class divides that govern everyone's lives.

PARAGRAPH 3

The development of Miss Havisham and Estella throughout the novel conveys how Victorian high-class society can greatly impact on the trajectory of one's life.[9] Both Pip and Estella are figures at the mercy of the malicious characters sculpted from the values of this time.[10] Thus, they themselves are shaped by these values into cruel and ignorant versions of themselves. Estella is moulded into a manipulative and callous woman by Miss Havisham as she uses Pip "to tease other admirers." Pip is similarly corrupted by Miss Havisham and Mr Jaggers to look down upon others and use them to his advantage, such as how he begins to scorn Joe for his "utterly preposterous" clothing. Dickens thus uses his characters to exemplify the shameful values that permeate Victorian high-class society. He furthers this notion by depicting the ravaging nature of this society on women through Estella and Miss Havisham. Miss Havisham's economic superiority affords her the stagnant yet opulent life that she has, allowing her to indulge in the manipulation of both Pip and Estella to exact "revenge on all the male sex." However, the lack of autonomy pressed upon Miss Havisham as an ageing, unmarried woman in the Victorian era is exemplified by Dickens through her reclusive lifestyle and "corpse-like," figure. Similarly, Estella is both restricted and enabled by the fraught ethics of upper-class London. Although she is "absorbed" into a lavish existence in London, she is simultaneously objectified and treated as a pawn to achieve Miss Havisham's revenge. As such, she is reduced to an embodiment of her mother's wealth and aspirations, reified in her statement "I and the Jewels."

9. It is useful to establish the main discussion point of a paragraph in a brief topic sentence.

10. This paragraph contains analysis of Miss Havisham, Estella, and Pip. In junior years of English, you may have been taught to focus on one character per body paragraph, but this approach is usually too simplistic by the time you get to your final years of English study. Instead, aim to incorporate multiple characters as has been done here – this enables you to draw more sophisticated conclusions by comparing and contrasting characters!

Estella's identity becomes intrinsically bound to the objects of affluence, causing her a life of misery. Thus, the author condemns the manner in which upper-class individuals and relationships are dominantly influenced by the materialistic, capitalistic, and amoral hegemony of Victorian society, leading to objectification, reification, and perpetual dissatisfaction.[11]

CONCLUSION
Dickens' *Great Expectations* traverses the significant extent to which the materialistic and economically determined constructs of a capitalist 19th century English society influences impressionable individuals and their relationships, accentuated through Pip, Estella, and Miss Havisham's pursuit for wealth, power, and admiration. These corrupt ideological authorities are depicted by Dickens to breed dissatisfaction, emphasising the satisfaction derived from a meritocratic lifestyle embodied by Joe. Thus, Charles Dickens highlights the substantial degree to which Victorian society shapes identity and relationships in the novel *Great Expectations*.

11. The end of your final body paragraph should almost sound like a conclusion, zooming out to consider the overall text and authorial intent. This ends the analysis on a strong note and sets the foundation for your conclusion to just wrap things up and secure you a high mark!

Essay Two

QUESTION: To what extent, and at what cost, are Pip's "great expectations" achieved?

ESSAY	COMMENTS
INTRODUCTION Charles Dickens' revolutionary novel *Great Expectations*[1] depicts the avaricious self-gratification and steep moral degradation that results from its protagonist Pip ascending to the upper class of Victorian society.[2] Through this portrayal, Dickens critically condemns the intrinsic greed and perverse ethics that dominated the upper echelons of 19th century England. As a bildungsroman, Pip's coming-of-age story, character development, and the three-part structure of the novel[3] are used by Dickens to portray a moral cautionary tale to his Victorian audience.	1. Make sure to establish the author, text, form, and title. 2. It's important to include some information to contextualise the novel in a time period or particular society even if the prompt doesn't explicitly ask for it. 3. Make sure to give the markers a brief outline of what you'll discuss in the body of your essay.
PARAGRAPH 1 Dickens sets up *Great Expectations* to foreshadow the ultimately negative consequences of Pip's rise in fortune, detailing the beginnings of corruption of a young boy by the amoral elite. Part 1 of Dickens' novel details Pip's burgeoning ambition as he receives his "great expectations." Pip is initially characterised as a morally-conscious young boy of low social status who becomes obsessed with hierarchal advancement after meeting Miss Havisham and Estella at Satis House.	

However, through the first-person, past-tense narration, Dickens intimates that Pip's "great expectations" aren't all that he dreams them to be, foreshadowing to the audience the "great changes" he will undergo as a gentleman in high society. The cost of his ultimately pyrrhic[4] achievement is similarly set up early in the novel by Dickens, who portrays the once honest and heartfelt relationship of Joe and Pip as becoming increasingly distant and transactional, as Pip wishes Joe had been more "genteelly brought up." Clothing, in particular shoes, is employed by Dickens as a motif of social class, as Pip begins to notice his "thick boots" and Joe's dirty work clothes. Ultimately, Dickens utilises Pip's characterisation and subsequent development early in the novel to to hint at the deleterious consequences of Pip's ambition and social advancement. Thus, even when Pip revels in supposedly achieving his "great expectations," readers are compelled to view his success with skepticism given the genuine relationships and morals he had to sacrifice.

PARAGRAPH 2
Although Pip achieves his "great expectations" and moves to London to become a gentleman, he is constantly reminded of his low upbringing and "commonly" status by those already inaugurated into bourgeoisie society. Bentley Drummle, a character foil to Pip,[5] acts to remind Pip of his low status. Drummle is a repugnant man who is not very intelligent or well-mannered, yet he is well-respected among the elite in society. Thus, Pip's ideals of what it means to be accepted into high society are questioned.

4. This is a great word to integrate in any essay that focuses on Pip's journey or the lessons he learns throughout the novel.
5. You don't need to summarise information about characters when you bring them up in your essay (as you are allowed to assume your marker has read the text!) but you may find it useful to make analytical remarks like this to comment on their role within the novel and how Dickens portrays them.

Dickens uses Drummle to depict the hypocrisies of the Victorian class system, which favours aristocracy and generational wealth, while also depicting the inadequacies of Pip's achievement of his new-found wealth. This is displayed in their conversation at the Blue Boar where Drummle alludes to Pip's working-class upbringing and they compare their shoes, "Mr Drummle looked at his boots and I looked at mine, and then Mr Drummle looked at my boots, and I looked at his," which is symbolic of their estimation of one another's social status. Similarly, by learning proper etiquette through Herbert, Pip must acknowledge that his "great expectations" are merely one element needed to achieve full acceptance in high-class society. Part 2 of *Great Expectations* continues Pip's journey to maturation and depicts him as he becomes embroiled in the life of high society, becoming judgemental and duplicitous. He is "mortified" by Joe's visit to London and also "patronise[s] Herbert" and thinks him less for his lack of wealth.[6] Thus, although Pip has achieved his goals, he becomes infected with self-importance and superiority while still not being allowed a true place in high-class society. As such, Dickens condemns the decline in morality and honesty that result from the rapacious pursuit for wealth and status, depicting the repercussions of Pip's rise in fortune.[7]

6. Make sure you have a substantial bank of quotes to draw from in your essays even if they're only short ones like this. Integrating precise quotes is often preferable to including huge chunks of the novel, so try to select the most important language and just paraphrase the rest (especially for Great Expectations which has lots of very wordy sentences that you don't want to waste time memorising!).

7. The end of this paragraph has a clear authorial intent statement ('Dickens condemns...') and directly addresses the core of the prompt so that the marker is left with no doubts about the relevance of our discussion.

PARAGRAPH 3

The most egregious loss resulting from Pip's pursuit for hierarchal advancement is his true and caring relationship with Joe, through which Dickens purports the moral teachings of the novel: that genuine relationships will ultimately provide a fulfilling life over the duplicitous pursuits of the bourgeoisie.[8] Pip's "great expectations" are ultimately stale as he comes to the realisation of the great casualty that is losing Joe. His coming-of-age arc is completed in part 3[9] of the novel as he realises his mistreatment of Joe and the resulting unhappiness of his upper-class life. Dickens claims this as the ultimate cost of Pip's pyrrhic endeavours for hierarchical ascension; the undeniable harm inflicted upon his genuine camaraderie with Joe. Pip suffers illness and large debts by the end of the novel, whilst Joe is rewarded with a satisfying marriage to Biddy and contentedness with his craft. Thus, Dickens reveals the true cost of unhindered ambition and advancement in Victorian society as a hollow and miserable pursuit. Pip must come to this realisation to achieve his happiness at the end of the novel, working hard to pay off his debts to Joe. Dickens intentionally leaves the end of the novel ambiguous with the "mists [in the village] rising," potentially alluding to Pip's happy future with Estella once he has repented for his immoral actions. Thus, Dickens suggests to his audience that the true cost of striving for economic gain and social superiority is a damaging detachment, the only remedy for which is the fulfilling endeavours of authentic friendship, generosity, and loyalty.

8. This is a strong interpretation of the novel that you could use for a wide variety of prompts. I'd highly recommend crafting your own versions of these sentences that you can adapt to suit different essays.

9. Although this essay happens to adopt a mostly chronological approach, in mostly focusing on each part of the novel in a separate paragraph, you don't have to stick to this. It happens to be a useful breakdown for this kind of essay prompt, but you should feel confident to draw evidence from elsewhere in the text whenever it is relevant to your discussion – don't think that you have to save an analysis of the novel's ending for your final body paragraph.

ESSAY	COMMENTS
CONCLUSION Ultimately, whilst Pip is successful in achieving the material wealth and status outlined in his "great expectations," his accomplishments are conclusively deemed to be hollow as they come at the significant cost of Pip's sense of identity and fulfilment derived from a kind-hearted, empathetic attitude and the emotionally authentic relationships in his life.[10] Thus, Dickens uses the cost of Pip's "great expectations" to iterate a moral cautionary tale to his 19th century audience.	10. Include a brief conclusion to summarise the content covered and more explicitly respond to the prompt. Don't forget to respond to the prompt! It's easier to forget than you would think, especially under the pressure of exam conditions.

Essay Three

QUESTION: How is the moral righteousness of the characters in Charles Dickens' *Great Expectations* reflected in their respective fates?

ESSAY	COMMENTS
INTRODUCTION Set in early 19th century England,[1] Charles Dickens' *Great Expectations* is rife with the contemplation of ethics and righteousness, ultimately becoming a "story of moral redemption" in which the genuinely virtuous characters are rewarded with satisfying, fulfilling fates and those who epitomise amorality are condemned by Dickens to detrimental fates. Dickens utilises the fates of the characters of Joe, Biddy, Miss Havisham, and Pip to enact a sense of moral justice in the story.	1. Make sure to establish the context of the novel early on, especially if it's pivotal to your argument.

PARAGRAPH 1

Joe Gargery and Biddy[2] are Dickens' exemplary examples of honourable moral values and genuine human connection, and as such are rewarded with a prevailing sense of contentment and satisfaction in the denouement of the narrative. From the very beginning of the novel, Pip's brother-in-law Joe is portrayed by Dickens as a guileless figure, characterised by his "good-natured companionship" with Pip and "sweet-tempered" attitude. Joe's gentle and affectionate demeanour is even manifested in his physical attributes, ascribed a soft sense of purity and virtue through his illustration as "a fair man, with curls of flaxen hair on each side of his smooth face." Furthermore, as the narrative progresses, Joe's passion for his craft as a blacksmith is established to be a genuinely fulfilling pursuit of merit, in congruence with his persistent support of Pip. Similarly, Biddy provides Pip with continuous assistance and patience when imparting "all her learning" to young Pip. She is kind to Pip even when he condescends and objectifies her in his pursuit to become a gentleman.[3] Dickens rewards Joe and Biddy's morally virtuous values with a sense of contentment at the end of the novel that other less ethical characters do not receive. Thus, Dickens commends the honest values upheld by both Joe and Biddy by rewarding them with an optimistic destiny.

2. Even though the essay prompt is asking us to focus on the characters in the novel, we also need to consider the thematic notions of moral righteousness and fate. Hence, this topic sentence outlines the key characters that will be discussed in this paragraph as well as the thematic concerns of honourable morality and achieving contentment.

3. This interpretation of Biddy can be a useful contrast against characters like Miss Havisham who redirect their fury at having been mistreated by people and channel it into mistreating others. You could draw similar distinctions between other characters based on their capacity for vengeance or forgiveness.

PARAGRAPH 2

Contrarily, the tragic fate of the "ghastly" and bitter Miss Havisham serves as a stark contrast to that of Joe and Biddy, as Dickens delineates the fatal consequences of moral corruption.[4] Miss Havisham relentlessly manipulates both Estella and Pip throughout the novel in her endeavour to "wreak revenge on all the male sex." Thus she subsequently raises Estella to be a cold-hearted object and exploits Pip's infantile naivety for her own ends. Miss Havisham's spiteful scheming in the hopes of achieving satisfaction is ultimately denounced by Dickens as a futile and inefficient means of seeking fulfilment, resulting in a stagnant lifestyle.[5] This immoral behaviour is punished by Dickens in her downfall that the end of the novel. Although she begs Pip for forgiveness, Dickens suggests that it is too late as she is engulfed by a "blazing" fire suffering severe injury and her eventual death. The disastrous fate that Miss Havisham suffers acts as a cautionary tale against corrupt moral values, as it is only after she has caused irreversible damage to the objectified figure of Estella and the exploited desires of Pip that she realises the detrimental effects of her malevolent games.

PARAGRAPH 3

While Pip succumbs to the corrupt lifestyle and values of the bourgeoisie throughout the novel, unlike Miss Havisham he learns from his mistakes and repents his actions before they can completely corrupt him.[6] As such, Pip suffers negative consequences but ultimately lives to find some sense of peace by the denouement of the novel.

4. Including a linking sentence between paragraphs is a great way to connect different paragraphs to continue your argument.

5. Notice that we're drawing clear links between the characters' fates and what Dickens is endorsing or condemning? This is a key element of morality in Victorian novels like Great Expectations, and if you are writing on a similar prompt, you should endeavour to make this same connection in your analysis. Don't just say 'Dickens condemns Miss Havisham' and 'Miss Havisham has a bad ending' as two separate ideas – connect the two and draw a conclusion about what Dickens is attempting to convey overall! In this case, his condemnation of Miss Havisham is also a repudiation of the vengeful attitudes she embodies.

6. This is an important distinction that separates Pip as a more sympathetic character than Miss Havisham and others. Here, it's also a useful bridge between the previous paragraph and this one, ensuring the essay flows nicely.

At the beginning the narrative, Pip has a prevailing sense of infantile innocence and moral integrity and is rewarded with fulfilment from his affectionate companionship with his "fellow sufferer" Joe. However, Pip's socio-economic advancements as he inherits a "handsome property" initiate a rapid decline in his virtuousness, instilling in him the capitalistic values of opulence and status over genuine human connection. As such, Dickens critiques[7] the corrupted values of the materialistic gentleman and condemns Pip to a turbulent downfall of immense debt and dissolution of his "great expectations." Yet, this tumultuous outcome is depicted by Dickens to inspire Pip's realisation of the damage caused by his distorted ethical views. After this realisation, Pip gains a newfound appreciation for the "old simplicity" associated with his fulfilling companionship to Joe, as well as a pure sense of gratitude towards Magwitch who selflessly provided Pip's grand "fortune" and took great pride in "making a gentleman." Thus, Pip begins his path to moral redemption, confiding in Magwitch, repairing his relationship with Joe, and "leaving arrogance and untruthfulness further and further behind." In the concluding imagery of the novel, Dickens ascribes a certain ambiguity to Pip's fate, as the evening mists rise on the marshes after his reunion with Estella. This evokes a further questioning of whether Dickens rewards Pip with an optimistic future or simply suggests an increasing clarity in his perspective after enduring the positive and negative consequences of his moral journey. Ultimately, through depicting both Pip's morally good and his morally questionable actions, Dickens suggests that moral redemption can change one's fate and lead to a fulfilling life.

7. Don't forget to link your arguments with either the prompt or the author's intentions, or better yet do both at the same time!

CONCLUSION Throughout the novel, Charles Dickens consistently navigates the complex nature of morality, illuminating the satisfaction achieved by genuine, empathetic characters and the often-merciless fates that punish the immoral actions of others. However, in evading the rigid constructs of good and bad, Dickens suggests a capacity for "moral redemption" that problematises seemingly objective ideals of Victorian society.[8]	8. Remember that you don't have to completely agree or disagree with a prompt/your argument. Including an alternate perspective can actually strengthen your argument by showing that you have cleverly considered the author's intentions from all perspectives. However, if you do this make sure you don't completely contradict your argument and you must refer to it throughout your essay, not just in the conclusion.

Essay Four

QUESTION: What role does Miss Havisham's character play in Charles Dickens' *Great Expectations*?

ESSAY	COMMENTS
INTRODUCTION Charles Dickens' 1861 novel *Great Expectations* follows the narrative of a young proletarian orphan named Pip who inherits a "handsome fortune"[1] from an anonymous benefactor and subsequently traverses the complex socio-economic milieu of 19th century England. Throughout the narrative, Pip encounters various eccentric characters from vastly differing positions on the Victorian social hierarchy, one of the most prominent being the "immensely rich and grim lady" Miss Havisham. Miss Havisham's character plays a pivotal role in manipulating Pip's desires, representing the destructive power of resentment, and the fatal consequences of a malevolent pursuit for revenge.	1. Including a short quote in the introduction can be valuable in highlighting your focus on certain elements of the text, but just remember that you shouldn't be doing any analysis in your introduction - save that for your body paragraphs where you can earn marks for it!

PARAGRAPH 1

The presence of Miss Havisham's character has an undeniably profound impact on Pip's development throughout the novel[2] as she exploits his infantile naivety in her vengeful pursuits for satisfaction. After making his first visit to Satis House Pip becomes infatuated by the prospect of becoming a gentleman in pursuit of Estella's affection, which Miss Havisham exploits as a tool to wreak "revenge on all the male sex." Miss Havisham's persistently questions Pip, repeatedly asking what he thinks of Estella and if "she grow[s] prettier and prettier." This accentuates her amoral intentions, to derive pleasure from the suffering of others, as evinced through Pip's unattainable aspirations of marrying Estella. This desire becomes synonymous with his desires for social advancement throughout the novel. Thus, Miss Havisham's dominant influence over Pip's romantic desire for the "irresistible" Estella contributes greatly to his burgeoning ambitions for wealth and status, leading to Pip's infectious immorality and greed that lead to his downfall.

PARAGRAPH 2

Moreover,[3] in raising Estella to be an objectified embodiment of beauty and wealth, Miss Havisham is characterised by Dickens as a challenge to upper-class morality as part of his broader critique on rigid social hierarchies in Victorian society. Estella is used as a "pawn" in Miss Havisham's manipulative games, trained by her adoptive mother to be "hard and thankless" and "never yielding either to anger or tenderness" in her pursuits to break the hearts of men.

2. Referring back to the prompt in the first sentence of your paragraph provides great context for your argument and helps the marker understand your point.

3. Connecting words like moreover, thus, furthermore, as such, etc. are really useful to connect between paragraphs and to help maintain the flow of the essay.

While Miss Havisham is successful in exploiting Pip's affections, the liberties that she is afforded to indulge in this manipulation ultimately results in the extreme objectification of Estella, who is reduced to an embodiment of her mother's wealth and aspirations devoid of any individual personality or autonomy. This becomes overtly evident in her statement "I and the jewels" in which the capitalisation of "jewels" and proximity of "I" as the pronoun of self-identification implies that Estella views herself as another valuable object. Therefore, Estella's identity becomes intrinsically bound to the objects of her affluence. Nonetheless, Estella's upbringing, raised with a "cold heart" without love or compassion results in her own inability to form genuine relationships, perpetuating the cycle of emotional damage.[4] As such, Miss Havisham herself also serves as a representation of restricted autonomy, as despite having ample material wealth, her liberty as an unmarried, ageing woman in 19th century England is depicted by Dickens to be constricted, symbolised in her "life of seclusion" and fraught female identity, left to "decay" in the "withering" ruins of her past relationship. Thus, Miss Havisham's manipulation and objectification of Estella depicts the destructive power of resentment and the negative consequences of building relationships devoid of honesty and kindness.

PARAGRAPH 3

Miss Havisham's character is symbolic of the perverse attitudes and values of 19th century Victorian society. She is a bitter and self-centred woman bent on revenge for being scorned on her wedding day. This revenge consumes her and leads to her tragic end as she is terribly injured by fire.

4. This paragraph draws connections between Estella's upbringing and how that reflects on Miss Havisham's character. This is yet another example of why it's valuable to analyse multiple characters within a body paragraph so that you can draw out more insights than if you were to only consider them in isolation.

Dickens utilises this tragedy as a moral consequence of her actions to Pip and Estella throughout the novel.[5] Miss Havisham is illustrated by Dickens as the epitome of bitterness and resentment. She remains "dressed in rich materials [...] all of white," with "a long white veil," and "bright jewels [that] sparkled on her neck and on her hands" that have all now become "faded and yellow," decaying along with her "corpse-like figure." Miss Havisham's inability to move forward is emphasised through these descriptions, ultimately resulting in her perpetual dissatisfaction and inevitable descent into illness and insanity towards the end of the novel.[6] Nonetheless, preceding her tragic imminent fate, Miss Havisham's insistence on being laid upon the dining table amongst the remnant "dust and mould" of her once "great" wedding cake after her death exemplifies her deep resentment. She arbitrarily endeavours to seek justice through the suffering and haunting of others, even at the cost of her own life. Inevitably, Dickens symbolically presents Miss Havisham's character and her withering estate as a cautionary tale of the perils of holding onto grievances and the necessity of embracing personal growth and forgiveness.[7]

5. As this is our final body paragraph, we can now draw together the different threads we've raised earlier in the essay to build up to our overarching interpretation by the end of this paragraph and the conclusion.

6. If you have a series of closely related quotes, you can incorporate lots of them and then analyse them all together as shown here. This is more efficient than adhering to a strict 'TEEL' structure or trying to analyse every single quote as you go.

7. This is another very strong interpretive statement that you could use and adapt for similar essays about Miss Havisham or the themes of revenge, change, or moral decay.

CONCLUSION
Thus, Miss Havisham plays a central role in the narrative path and themes of Dickens' *Great Expectations*, shaping the lives of both Pip and Estella as well as serving to symbolise the perilous consequences of malicious resentment.